Bits, Bytes and Buzzwords:

Understanding Small Business Computers

Bits, Bytes and Buzzwords:

Understanding Small Business Computers

Mark Garetz

dilithium Press
Beaverton, Oregon

10 9 8 7 6 5 4 3 2 1

Library of Congress Cataloging in Publication Data

Garetz, Mark, 1953-
    Bits, bytes, and buzzwords.

    Includes index.
    1. Small business – Data processing.
2. Microcomputers. I. Title. II. Title: Understanding small business computers.
HF5548.2.G35 1983   001.64   82-25238
ISBN 0-88056-111-4

Printed in the United States of America

dilithium Press
8285 S.W. Nimbus, Suite 151
Beaverton, Oregon 97005

Contents

Introduction

Welcome to the first book about computers that is going to make sense to you! We are going to explain to you, in simple everyday language, what computers are all about. We're not going to bore or confuse you with lots of meaningless information useful only to those who design or fix computers. We're going to tell you only what you need to know and nothing more. This book is for you: the individual who is thinking of buying or has just bought a computer system to *get some work done!* You don't want a computer to play games with, you want it to increase your productivity. But the thought of buying a computer for your office, or of making a trip to the local computer store, may scare you.

That's where this book comes in. By taking the mystery out of computers, and by defining the sometimes confusing "buzzwords" you'll encounter, this book will enable you to make a much more intelligent buying decision: you won't be scared. Hopefully, you will be reading this book *before* you buy your computer; but if not, you can still learn a lot from this book. If you should learn that you've made a poor choice in buying your first computer, you'll be wiser the next time around (and if you made a poor choice, there *will* be a next time!).

Computers are not magic, but they can often seem to be. By compressing hours of human labor into seconds of computer time, this universal tool increases productivity, streamlines operations and expedites paperwork. Computers shouldn't be intimidating. Deep down in their little silicon hearts, all they really care about is solving problems for humans. That seems pretty friendly. By the end of this book, you'll feel pretty friendly towards computers, too.

About This Book

This book is organized into five sections. In the first four sections, we are going to explain computer systems to you. Notice that we used the phrase *computer system* instead of just *computer*. That's because any useful computer setup consists of more than just the basic computer. It takes many accessories to make the whole thing work, and we're going to tell you all about those, too. Our explanations will be given with an eye towards your actual purchase of a computer system. At the end of the first four sections, we will recap what you've learned and give you some pointers on what to do when you walk into that computer store to buy a computer.

The last section of this book is a glossary that contains definitions of words and phrases that will be introduced in the rest of the book. That is not to say that we won't explain these new terms as we introduce them, but the glossary will serve as a handy reference in case you forget what something means. When a new phrase or word is first introduced in this book, it will be printed in boldface like this: **buzzword**.

You have probably heard the term "buzzword" many times before. It refers to a word that has some mystical meaning, at least as far as computer people are concerned. Buzzwords really don't have any special significance other than that they are usually abbreviated ways of saying something complex, just like jargon in any field.

Before We Get Started — What Can the Computer Do for Me?

Since you're reading this book, someone or something has put the notion into your head that a small computer might be useful around the office or workplace. But you may not be sure just what these marvels can do for you.

What if we told you that a typical small business computer could make writing reports and correspondence a breeze, be a perfect typist, check your spelling, fine tune your business plan, simplify your accounting tasks, keep track of loads of information about your customers (or anything) and be able to instantly sort through it and retrieve something for you, handle your inventory, print your invoices, run off a mailing list, and let you blast Klingons to the other side of the galaxy (in your spare time, of course)? Do you think you could make use of one? We think you could, too.

Really, it all boils down to this: Computers are intended to make your work (and therefore, your life) easier. And by doing that, you can get more work done in the same amount of time.

WOULD YOU MIND BEING
A LITTLE MORE SPECIFIC?

Not at all. You'd probably like to know in a little more detail what kinds of things a computer can do for you.

First of all, we said that a computer could make writing easier for you. Imagine being able to type correspondence on a TV-like screen. As you type, the sentences and paragraphs appear on the screen. Make a mistake? Press a single key and letters, words, sentences or even whole blocks of text disappear. Want to shift a few paragraphs around? Press a few more keys and completely reorganize your text. Rather have it doublespaced? Press another key and everything you've already typed is now magically transformed to doublespacing. You can change your margins just as easily.

Finished composing your letter? Want it checked for spelling and grammar? Press another key and in a flash you'll see all the misspelled words and any possible grammatical errors. Press a few more keys and correct them all.

Time to put the letter on paper? Press another key and it will be typed many times faster than the best typist, and without a single error. Don't like the way that paragraph sounds after all? A few more keystrokes and you can change and print it all again.

It sounds like magic and wizardry, but it's not. It's one of the *easier* tasks for that small wonder to accomplish. It's called **word processing**. If you think about it, everything we just described had to do with processing words. Word processing can certainly make your life (or your secretary's) a lot easier.

Would you like to build a financial model of your business (or department) where all the various numbers and calculations are all interrelated? You change one number and all the rest could be affected. If you tried it on paper, it could take hours, even days, to try

out a few combinations. But the computer can perform thousands of complex calculations and display
the results in a wink of the eye. You can now play
"what-if" games that would otherwise wear the keys on
your calculator down to the nub from constant use.
For example: What if your sales decreased by 10%
over the next six months while your overhead in-
creased 8% and wages remained constant? Could you
still make a profit? What if you went 35% over budget
on developing your new widget? Could you still charge
$1.95 for it? What if you reduced the wholesale
margins? Spent a little more on advertising?

Does this sound like something you could use? This
type of operation is called **financial modeling** or **forecasting** and is one of the more popular uses for the
small business computer.

One of the primary purposes of the computer in
business has always been to help with accounting, billing and invoicing tasks. You've known for a long time
that your utility bills, and credit card and bank statements were all calculated and printed by computers.
The big guys have been using them almost since the
computer was invented. Now you can afford to use a
small business computer to perform the same jobs for
yourself.

Imagine being able to know instantly what items
you have in stock, what each item costs you, and how
much you sell it for. Or being reminded automatically
when it's time to reorder a specific item. You can find
out the value of your inventory in an instant. The computer can even be your cash register. These inventory
control functions are another example of the many
uses of the small business computer.

When you take an order for an item, the order can be
entered directly into the computer. Stock levels can be
checked instantly and, if the item is in stock, an invoice and shipping tag can be printed and stock levels
reduced automatically. If the item is out of stock, a
backorder notice is printed. When the item comes in,

the computer will know that someone has it on back-order, and an invoice and shipping tag will be printed. Meanwhile, all the information about that transaction (and all others) has been recorded and filed away by the computer. The computer stores the customer's name and address, the items purchased, the amount spent, the invoice number and so on.

Suppose a new item comes in that may be of interest to some of your customers that bought similar items in the past. Furthermore, suppose this new item is fairly expensive. You could ask the computer to print out a mailing list of all customers who have purchased similar items in the last six months, spent an average of fifty dollars or more per order, and live in your state. The computer will happily comply. You could just as easily have asked the computer to tell you how many of a particular item you sold last month or last year.

Once you have this broad base of data (called a **data base**), you can sort through it and retrieve any or all of it at will. You can probably think of many uses for this type of capability; it's a very common application of the small business computer.

Finally you just might want to relax and command a starship through the galaxy for what's left of your lunch hour (and hope the Klingons don't eat you for lunch!).

With a small business computer, all of this magic is at your fingertips.

MIGHT IT BE TOO COMPLICATED
FOR ME TO USE?

Not at all. You don't have to be a computer whiz to make today's small business computer do your bidding. In fact, computers are now easier and simpler to use than ever before. Most tasks actually help you along. Forget what comes next? A keystroke can bring up a bit of help. Not enough? Another keystroke and some more help appears. Still not enough? A few more keystrokes and you've got a whole course on the subject. With a little training, anyone (including you!) can use a small computer.

A MYTH ABOUT SMALL BUSINESS COMPUTERS

The biggest myth about computers is that they replace people. Never happens. What does happen is that the person using the computer gets more work done, more efficiently and better than ever before. This means that person can handle more work, not less, but the work is now much easier. Don't buy a computer because you think you can replace your bookkeeper. What will happen is this: your book-keeper will handle twice as many accounts. Your book-keeper will need to handle twice as many accounts because your whole operation will be running more ef-ficiently and doing much more business.

Using computers leads to growth, because busi-nesses that operate better tend to grow.

Now that you're convinced you need a small busi-ness computer, you're ready to learn all about what makes them tick. Then you can make intelligent deci-sions about the kind of computer you need.

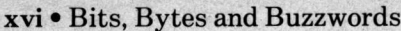

Section 1

The Basic Computer System

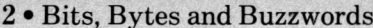

Chapter One

What Is a Computer System?

There is mass confusion about the difference between a computer and a computer system. A computer is more correctly just the brains of the outfit. It just computes. It can't tell you anything about what it's doing, nor can you tell it what to do. What good is a computer then? Not much. That's why you need a computer **system** to get your jobs done.

Computer systems start with the basic computer and combine it with other devices that allow it to talk to you and you to it. It's sort of like a stereo system. If you just had an amplifier, you could turn it on, but you wouldn't hear anything until you added speakers. Even then you wouldn't hear anything until you added a turntable and a record. Most people think of the computer and the computer system as one and the same; people say "computer" when they mean "computer system." You will probably find those two terms used interchangeably throughout this book, mainly because it's easier to say "computer" than "computer system."

Well then, what makes up a computer system? Just as better stereo systems combine different components (amplifier, turntable, speakers, etc.) into a well integrated system, better computer systems are also made up of individual components. A computer system includes

- **Hardware**, which is the machine itself;
- **Software**, which are the instructions that tell the machine how to perform a particular task, such as accounting or word processing;
- **Input** and **Output Devices** that allow the computer to communicate with the operator or other computers; and most importantly,
- **You**, the person who, after some training and a few hours spent with instruction manuals, can make the whole system come to life and do your bidding.

It is important to remember that all computer systems must contain these four elements in order to function at all, let alone perform useful work.

HOW DO THE PARTS OF A COMPUTER SYSTEM WORK WITH EACH OTHER?

The various parts of a computer system work together to complete tasks in much the same way that the various parts of a human being work together to complete tasks. We humans use our five senses (some use six) to gather information from our surroundings; the brain processes this information by comparing it to related experiences stored in our memory, and directs the body to take appropriate action based on this new sensory information and our previous experiences. For example, if you are cooking a nice steak and all of a sudden you smell smoke, that's an **input** to the brain (your nose is the input device). The brain then seeks out more information. If the steak is burning and causing the smoke, your brain's **program** reminds you that burnt steak has never tasted very good in the past, and probably won't in this instance either! So the brain then directs an **output** device—in this case your arm—to take the steak off the stove. If the steak wasn't on fire, your brain would direct your body to continue the search for the source of the smoke. If the sofa's on fire, your brain's program would cause you to run for the fire extinguisher, which, hopefully, your brain's program knows how to operate.

Computers work in a similar way. They have **input devices** (such as a keyboard) that let you put information into the computer, a "brain" or **central processor unit** (called a **CPU** for short), a program or programs (also known as software) that tells the computer what to do with the information it receives from the input devices, and finally, **output devices** (such as a TV-like screen) that let the computer communicate with you. These various input and output devices (**I/O devices** for short) are called **peripherals**, which is just a fancy computer term for "accessories."

So much for grand concepts. Now let's get specific and see how these various computer components work together.

THE MAINFRAME

The **mainframe** is the brain of the computer system. It gets its name from the fact that it is a frame, usually made out of metal, that houses the main functions of the computer system: main frame. The term is really a hold-over from the days when most computer systems occupied the space of several rooms and there really was a *main* frame, and several secondary frames as well. With today's modern silicon wizardry, only one frame is usually needed, but it is still called the mainframe anyway.

The mainframe contains the brain of the outfit, and much like a human brain, there are several parts that make up this brain. Each part is a complete electronic circuit whose components are mounted on a **circuit board** (see Figure 1.1).

These circuit boards include lots of electronic parts. The most common part is called an **integrated circuit** (**IC** for short); an example is shown in Figure 1.2. Each IC performs a specific function on the circuit board

Figure 1.1 A circuit board. *Courtesy of CompuPro.*

Figure 1.2 An IC (integrated circuit).
Courtesy of Intel Corporation.

(some more complex than others) and the typical business level computer will have dozens, or even hundreds, of these ICs.

The circuit board provides a stable mounting surface for the ICs and also provides electrical paths (called **traces**) that connect the ICs together. Usually, each circuit board handles a specific task within the mainframe, and depending on the tasks that a given computer is designed to do, it may have from one to many dozen of these circuit boards. Typically, there will be separate circuit boards for the

- **Central Processing Unit**, which performs calculations and various logical operations;
- **Memory**, which is used to store the programs and information that the computer needs to operate;
- **Input/Output** or **I/O** circuitry, which allows the computer to communicate with its various I/O devices;
- **Special Function Boards**, which help the computer complete tasks faster or more efficiently, and also to perform those tasks that don't fit neatly into any one general category (such as telling the time); and the
- **Power Supply**, which is the computer's energy source.

These are all the pieces that make up the computer's brain, but since your brain would be useless if you didn't have your head to put it in, we also need something to house all these electronic gizmos. This housing is called the **computer enclosure** and it, along with the brainy boards just discussed, make up the main frame. Be aware of the distinction here between the enclosure itself and the mainframe; it's easy to get them confused because the enclosure is all you see of the mainframe. Remember that the mainframe consists of the enclosure *and* all those goodies inside; a computer enclosure by itself will not compute.

We will discuss the CPU, memory, I/O boards, computer enclosure and peripherals in more detail in the following chapters. Right now we will tell you about the various ways that computer systems are packaged.

STYLES OF COMPUTERS –
HOW THEY ARE PACKAGED

Computers come in three basic types. The first type is one where the entire computer (CPU, memory and I/O interfaces) is all contained on one (usually large) circuit board. These computers are generally called **single-board computers** and are not expandable. You can never add any more features to the single-board computer after you buy it. It's kind of like buying a photo copier that can handle only 8½×11-inch paper; if the need arises to make 11×17-inch copies, you need a new copier. The old one cannot be **up-graded** to handle the larger size paper. (Up-grading is a term used by salespeople and manufacturers. It describes the process of making a hardware change to an existing computer so that it can do even more wonderful things than it could when you bought it.)

The second type of computer is one where the computer is all contained on one circuit board, but the manufacturer has left some empty places (usually called **slots**) to plug in added functions. There isn't really any established name for this type of computer configuration, but for purposes of this book, we'll call it a **semi-modular** computer. This is because part of the computer configuration is fixed and part can be changed by adding certain modules.

The third type (and the one we prefer) is the completely modular computer. As the name implies, the modular computer has no main circuit board at all; each of the functions are contained on separate circuit boards. For example, the CPU, memory and I/O functions each have their own circuit board. Thus, when it becomes time to change to a snazzier CPU (one that might allow more secretaries to do word processing on the same computer, for instance), only the CPU module needs to be replaced; the rest of the system remains intact.

Now, let's discuss these three types in a little more detail:

The Single-Board Computer

As we mentioned earlier, the single-board computer has all the necessary circuitry to do basic computing tasks contained on one circuit board. These computers are packaged in two basic configurations. The first is the **all-in-one** computer. This type of computer contains everything you need to start computing all contained in one package. The computer, keyboard, screen and disk drives are all combined into one table-top package (or sometimes a small group of packages that are purchased as a whole). Sometimes these are designed to be portable as well.

Examples of current all-in-one computers are pictured in Figures 1.3 through 1.5. Shown here are the North Star Advantage, the Xerox 820 and the Osborne 1. The North Star computer has everything combined into one package while the Xerox computer has three smaller packages that all connect together. This does not make the Xerox computer modular; you still get Xerox's choice of screen, keyboard and computer. The Osborne 1 is an example of an all-in-one unit that is designed to be portable.

The second type of single-board computer is very similar to the all-in-one computers, except that the manufacturer lets you decide what kind of keyboard and screen you like, which means that you have to buy them separately. (Keyboard/screen combinations are called **terminals**; we'll cover them later in a chapter all their own.) Figure 1.6 shows an Altos computer, which is an example of a single board computer that only needs a terminal to operate.

Figure 1.3 North Star Advantage Computer.
Courtesy of North Star.

Figure 1.4 Xerox 820 Computer. *Courtesy of Xerox.*

Figure 1.5 Osborne 1 Computer.
Courtesy of Osborne Computers.

The Pros and Cons of Single-Board Computers

Single-board computers can be a great place to start computing (most "home" computers are single-board computers), but we generally don't recommend them for serious business computing. If you are certain that your computing needs will never outgrow the capabilities of the single-board computer, then that may be your best choice (the rest of the book will help you make that decision). The cost to get started in computing can be much lower with the single-board systems than for others, which makes them very attractive to the first time computer buyer. But remember that the single-board computer's main disadvantage is its lack of expandability. Here's something to consider: our experience has shown that most people fail to adequately estimate their computing needs, and are

Figure 1.6 Altos Computer. *Courtesy of Altos Computers.*

soon disappointed because the single-board computer they just bought needs to be replaced after only a few months of use.

The Semi-modular Computer

The semi-modular computer spans a whole range of products. These are computers that come with most of the components chosen for you (like what type of CPU), but allow some expansion. The degree of expandability varies widely; some allow almost the entire machine to be changed, while others allow only the addition of a few options. The latter example is by far the most common. The IBM PC (shown in Figure 1.7

Figure 1.7 IBM PC with lid off showing expansion slots.
Courtesy of Xedex.

with its cover removed) is a good example of a semi-modular computer. Notice that there is quite a bit of circuitry on the main circuit board, but there are five slots in the back that allow more features to be added. The main board contains the CPU and memory, while the slots allow you to add a color display, more memory and boards allowing the use of different kinds of peripherals. Other popular semi-modular computers include the Apple II and III, and the Zenith Z-100.

The Pros and Cons of Semi-modular Computers

Semi-modular computers can be a good compromise between a single-board computer and a completely modular computer. They will generally be somewhat more expensive than single-board computers, and will vary widely in their degree of expandability. The advantages are that you can tailor the computer to your needs more precisely and they provide some insurance against outgrowing the computer's capabilities. The disadvantages are that while the semi-modular computers can be expanded, their expandability is limited and often isn't enough. These computers are designed to perform well in a certain range of applications and may not be flexible enough to change with you as your needs change. The cost of a really flexible semi-modular computer may be as much as a truly modular computer anyway.

The Modular Computer

If you haven't been able to figure it out by now, the type of computer that we think is the best buy for the serious business computer user is the modular computer. This type of computer can be changed and up-graded at will (if you buy the right one, and we'll help you make the right choice). The modular computer has an enclosure that generally resembles a plain box. In the bottom of the enclosure is a special circuit board called a **motherboard**. We won't go into too much detail about the motherboard right now (that's covered in another chapter), but all you need to know for now is that the motherboard provides a means of connecting the various modules together. (These modules are called **daughter boards**.) The modular computer will usually come with enough daughter boards to start you computing; all you need to do is add the terminal of your choice. This package may be put together (**integrated**) by the computer store that you're dealing with, or it may come that way from the manufacturer (**pre-integrated**). In any case, you should be able to buy a computer system that's right for your needs now, but be able to completely change the sys-tem when your needs change, at a much lower cost than getting rid of your previous computer.

An example of a modular computer is shown in Fig-ure 1.8. This computer, manufactured by CompuPro, is what is known as an **IEEE 696/S-100** computer. That's a fancy phrase for saying that this computer uses a standard method for connecting the daughter

Figure 1.8 CompuPro Computer with lid off.
Courtesy of CompuPro.

boards together, and that you are not locked into buying all the modules of this system from one manufacturer. IEEE 696/S-100 computers are the most popular among modular computer manufacturers, and we recommend it highly.

The Pros and Cons of Modular Computers

There are many advantages to buying a modular computer, the biggest being that your investment is protected against obsolescence. A properly designed modular computer can start out with just one person doing word-processing and some financial forecasting, and expand to handle the needs of an entire office. The other main advantage is that you can buy the system that exactly fits your computing needs (and not be afraid that you didn't estimate them correctly). You won't have to compromise by taking all the choices a manufacturer has made for you, because you can make all the choices yourself. Don't let that scare you: by the time you finish this book, you'll be able to make those choices wisely.

The two main disadvantages of modular computers are the complexity of deciding what modules to buy (this book and a good dealer should minimize that disadvantage), and cost. A modular computer system will generally cost more at the outset than a single-board or semi-modular computer. But the cost is usually much less over the long run, because the system can grow with you. You won't have to buy a new computer.

WHAT HAVE YOU LEARNED SO FAR?

You learned about the basic parts of a computer system and how they work together to complete tasks, much like the various parts of the human body work together to get things done. And you've also learned about the three basic types of computer configurations, and that we think a modular IEEE 696/S-100 computer system is the best choice of the three. That wasn't too hard, was it?

Let's continue now and examine the various parts of the computer system in more detail. In the following chapters, we're going to talk about the various computer boards as if they are parts of a modular system, not just because we feel that modular systems are best, but because it's easier to think about them as modules.

Chapter Two

The CPU Board

As you learned in Chapter One, CPU is an abbreviation for central processing unit, and it is really the brains of the outfit. The CPU board will usually contain at least one CPU chip. The CPU chip is the heart of the CPU board and it is usually a big IC having forty or more little legs. Inside the IC package is the actual piece of silicon that you often see balanced on the end of someone's finger (like in Figure 2.1). While that little chip has a lot of power, it needs many other ICs to allow it to "talk" to the rest of the computer system. That's where the rest of the circuitry on the CPU board comes in. A typical CPU board is shown in Figure 2.2. Note the rather large IC; that's the CPU chip.

WHAT DOES THE CPU DO?

The CPU is like the controller of a large railroad yard. The yard controller is in charge of all the boxcars that come in and go out of the yard. He must make sure that the right boxcars get connected together in the right order and that they leave on the right tracks. Basically, the yard controller is processing information: each boxcar is a unit of information, and that information must be moved from place to place. He makes decisions based on the schedules and shipping orders (the program) and groups the boxcars (informa-

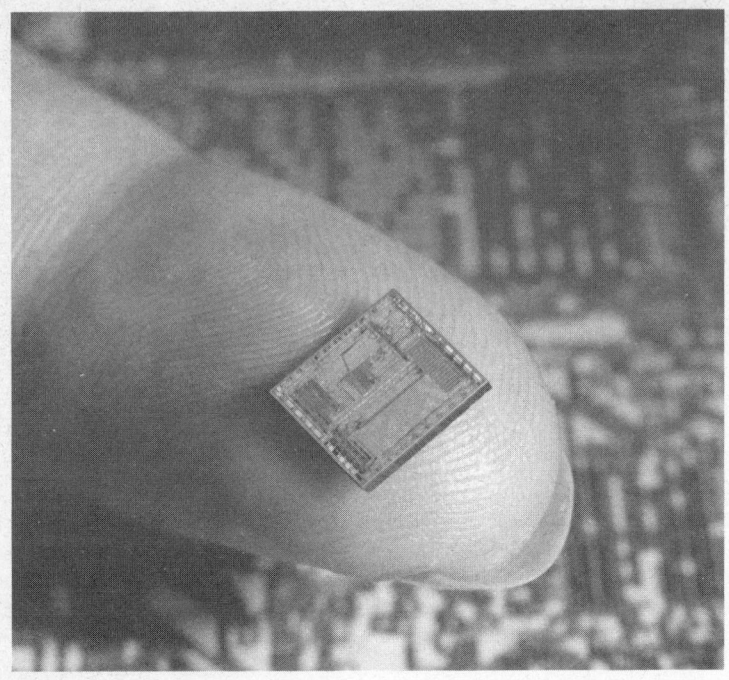

Figure 2.1 The classic picture of a silicon chip balanced on the end of someone's finger. *Courtesy of Intel Corporation.*

Figure 2.2 CPU board (CPU-Z). *Courtesy of CompuPro.*

tion) accordingly. Calculations must be made based on the information at hand, swtiches must be thrown at the right time so that the boxcars go where they should, and the trains don't run into each other. Of course, the yard controller sits in a high tower and never actually moves boxcars directly. Switching engines are assigned to do that task. The yard controller directs the flow of boxcars.

The CPU in a computer system performs much the same tasks as the railroad yard controller: directing the flow of information around the computer system. The CPU makes decisions based on its program and the data it is handling. In addition to elementary decision-making and directing the flow of information, the CPU can also perform various arithmetic and "logical" functions on the data. The arithmetic functions are the common add and subtract functions that you are already familiar with. We don't really need to discuss the logical functions, except to say that they help the CPU make its decisions.

ALL CPU CHIPS ARE NOT CREATED EQUAL

Because CPU chips are made by a whole lot of different IC manufacturers, each manufacturer tries to make its CPU chip more complicated than the ones that came before it. IC manufacturers (and CPU board manufacturers) call their newest baby "more powerful" than the ones that came before, and what that means can vary widely. Let's start at the beginning of microcomputer time: 1973.

That was the year when Intel introduced the first real CPU chip, the 8080. Even though this was the first CPU on a chip, many hundreds of thousands of them are still in use today. Later, Intel introduced the 8085, which didn't have any more computing power than the 8080, but could compute much faster. Soon after, a company called Zilog introduced a chip called the Z-80 which was the answer to everyone's dreams. It did everything the 8080 did, and a whole lot more. Most computer manufacturers switched immediately to the Z-80, and it is still in wide-spread use today.

The 8080, 8085 and Z-80 chips belong in the group known as **8 Bit Processors**. This is because they handle information 8 bits at a time. A **bit** is computer lingo for *b*inary dig*it*. It is the most basic piece of information that a computer can handle. A binary digit is either a 0 or a 1 and it can only represent two conditions, on or off. To represent more complex conditions, such as somewhere between on and off, more bits need to be grouped together. The more bits that are grouped together, the more possible combinations there are. The most common number of bits that are grouped together is eight. With eight bits, you can represent 256 different values or codes. Since the grouping of eight bits is so common, a name has been given to the group: the **byte**. The term byte refers to a group of eight bits. Don't worry about remembering this technical talk about bits and bytes; the most important thing to remember is that one byte is used to represent one **character** such as a letter, space or punctuation mark.

Back to CPUs. As we said before, the 8080, 8085 and Z-80 are all eight bit CPUs. The newer generation of CPU chips are known as **16 Bit Processors**. In general, they are more powerful than their eight bit counterparts. If you're moving data around inside a computer, it stands to reason that a CPU that moves 16 bits of data at a time can be twice as efficient as a CPU that moves 8 bits at a time. Sixteen bit CPUs are becoming more popular all the time. Examples of 16 bit CPUs are the 8088, 8086, 68000, 16032 and the 80286.

This is not to say that 16 bit CPUs are necessarily better than 8 bit CPUs, as you'll see in the next section.

8 OR 16 BITS, WHICH DO I WANT?

This is a tough question to answer. In general, an 8 bit system is fine for a one person (**single-user**) computer, meaning that only one person will be using the computer at a time. A 16 bit computer is more desirable for a system where more than one person will be using the computer at the same time (more commonly known as a **multi-user system**).

One reason why we like the modular computer approach is that you might want to start off with an 8 bit CPU, and later change to 16 bit CPU as your computing needs grow.

A trend in 16 bit computer systems is to include an 8 bit processor in addition to the 16 bit processor. The idea is to allow 16 bit operation when needed, but retain the ability to use older 8 bit programs (more of which exist at the current time than 16 bit programs). The first processor card to include a 16 bit and an 8 bit CPU was the CompuPro CPU 8085/88; it is shown in Figure 2.3. Note the two large ICs towards the right; these are the two CPUs.

Figure 2.3 CompuPro CPU 8085/88 board.
Courtesy of CompuPro.

IF 8 BITS IS FINE FOR ME, DO I REALLY NEED A Z-80?

We said earlier that the Z-80 was supposed to be the answer to everyone's dreams. The Z-80 is a more powerful 8 bit CPU than the 8085 or 8080, but let's examine that statement a little more closely. The Z-80 is more powerful because it not only does the exact same things as an 8085, but does even more. It's like a microwave oven. The earlier microwave ovens had only one power setting: full. Newer microwave ovens have a whole range of power settings, from very low to full. If we were to write a recipe that depended on cooking something at half power, only people with newer units could use the recipe. But if we wrote our recipe so that it used only the full power setting, everyone could use it regardless of the age of their oven.

The point is that most of the programs (recipes) in existence are written for the 8080, and do not take advantage of the extra power built into the Z-80. The reason is obvious: programmers want to sell their programs to as many people as possible, and making them work only with the Z-80 would exclude hundreds of thousands of potential customers who own 8080 and 8085-based computers.

WHAT HAVE YOU LEARNED SO FAR?

You learned that the CPU is the brains of the outfit, and some brains are better than others. The CPU chip itself needs the help of many other ICs to make it actually work in the computer system; they all usually live on the CPU board. The CPU performs the function of controlling the flow of information around the computer system and it can make decisions based on that information. It can also perform arithmetic and logical functions on that information.

You also learned the difference between 8 bit and 16 bit CPUs (and in the process you learned about bits and bytes). Computers based on 8 bit CPUs are generally fine for single-user operation, but 16 bit computers are better for multi-user applications.

And lastly, you learned that you probably don't really need a Z-80 because there aren't many programs that exploit its advantages. That doesn't mean you should shy away from a Z-80-based computer, just don't rule out an 8085-based computer because it doesn't have a Z-80 in it.

Chapter Three

Memory

In Chapter Two, you learned that a CPU controls the flow of information in the computer system. That information is contained in the computer's memory. This chapter explains all about memory.

We humans absorb information and store it in our memory; we can refer to it as we need it (assuming we don't forget it). Computers use their memory in much the same way. The text of a letter that you enter into the computer is stored in memory, but the program that tells the computer how to get the text into memory, and also what to do with it once it's there, is also stored in memory. In simpler terms, both information and programs are contained in a computer's memory. For example, you have quite a few phone numbers in your memory, and you also remember how to dial the phone. The phone numbers are the data you need to reach someone, but what to do with the numbers is contained in your phone dialing program. They are both contained in your memory.

Before we discuss the computer's memory, it might be a good idea to review some information from the previous chapter, specifically what bits and bytes are, and what they mean to us.

A bit is the most basic piece of information a computer can handle. *Bit* is a combination of the two words *binary digit*. A binary digit can be either a 0 (zero) or a 1 (one). Therefore, a bit can represent two possibilities, yes or no. To represent more complex possibilities (such as "almost yes") many bits are grouped together. The more bits that are grouped together, the more complex a possibility you can represent.

The most common number of bits in a group is eight, and this group of eight bits is called a byte. Computers use one byte to represent one character, such as a letter of the alphabet, a number, a space or a punctuation mark. A computer's memory is measured in bytes, but let's relate that measurement to something we can grasp easily: There are approximately 1500 characters on a typewritten, double-spaced page of text, so 1500 bytes would be required to store a page's worth of information.

Now that we've got a feel for what a byte is (and what it means to us) let's proceed:

The memory of a computer system is called **RAM**; that stands for Random Access Memory. The term "random access" refers to the fact that any byte in the memory can be accessed at random, or in no particular order. The first computer memories were serial access memories, which meant that you might have to access a whole sequence of bytes before getting to the one you wanted. Serial access memories are not used at all today, because random access memories are clearly more efficient.

The more RAM a computer has, the more efficient it is. It can hold bigger programs and more data at the same time. The amount of RAM in a computer system is specified in bytes. The typical single-user computer system may contain upwards of 64,000 bytes of RAM. Since it's inconvenient to write out large numbers like 64,000, you'll often see the abbreviation **K bytes** (kilobytes). One K byte equals 1024 bytes, so a computer with 64K bytes of RAM actually contains 65,536 bytes of RAM ($64 \times 1024 = 65,536$). A typical multi-user computer system might contain 512K bytes of RAM.

Now is a good time to touch briefly on a subject that confuses most newcomers to computers. The RAM in a computer is the only memory that the CPU can "talk to" directly. Information that the computer needs (programs and data) is not stored permanently in its RAM. Instead, the information is stored "permanently" on something called a **mass storage system**. The most common mass storage system (and the one you've probably heard of) is the floppy disk system. Without getting ahead of ourselves too much (mass storage systems will be covered in detail in a subsequent chapter), the mass storage system stores the data for use by the computer, but the computer must first transfer the data to its RAM before it can be used. In a nutshell, the memory of a computer (RAM) should not be confused with the mass storage system even though they are both "memory." The mass storage system stores data for future use by the computer, but the RAM is involved in the moment to moment operation of the computer.

The information stored in a computer's RAM will be lost when power to the computer goes away (when you turn it off). Memory that loses its data when power goes away is called **volatile**. The data in a mass storage system is **non-volatile** because it remains after power goes away.

HOW MUCH MEMORY DO I NEED?

To the first microcomputer systems, 256 bytes was a lot of memory, and 8K bytes was an enormous amount (memory was expensive back then). Nowadays, the minimum amount of memory a computer should have is 64K bytes. A lot of applications require the use of more than 64K, such as multi-user systems. Multi-user systems would use about 64K bytes per user. Sixteen bit systems also require larger amounts of memory; 128K byte systems are not uncommon. The actual amount of memory you need depends largely on the things you want your computer to do. Your computer dealer should be able to determine the right amount of memory for you.

A typical memory board that contains 128K bytes of RAM is shown in Figure 3.1.

Figure 3.1 Memory board (RAM 21). *Courtesy of CompuPro.*

CAN I ADD MORE MEMORY TO MY COMPUTER LATER?

That depends on the type of computer that you buy. A single-board computer generally comes with the maximum amount of memory it can have. A modular system can usually take much more memory than it comes with initially. A computer that comes with 64K bytes of RAM, but is expandable to 1 **Megabyte** of RAM, can have that much more RAM added to it. (A megabyte is approximately 1 million bytes or 1024K bytes.)

TYPES OF MEMORY – STATIC VS. DYNAMIC

There are two basic types of memory technology in use today: static and dynamic. Without getting too technical, here is the difference. A static memory retains its data as long as power is still on. A dynamic memory retains its data only for a short while (about two thousandths of a second). It needs to be "refreshed" about 500 times a second so that the data will be there when you need it.

The biggest advantage of dynamic memory over static memory is that it takes less space to build a dynamic memory IC than a static memory IC. This means that dynamic memories are usually more dense (meaning they have more bits) than static memories, and the cost per bit is lower. However, the complications of the refreshing operation usually outweigh this advantage. This is especially true in a modular environment.

Dynamic memories are fine in single-board and semi-modular systems, but are not recommended for modular systems.

WHAT HAVE YOU LEARNED SO FAR?

You learned that the computer's memory contains all the information that it needs to do its work. It contains both programs and data, and when you turn off the power, everything in the memory is lost. You also learned not to confuse the computer's RAM with the type of storage that a mass storage device provides.

You know that the basic computer system should contain at least 64K bytes of RAM, and you learned what a K byte and a M (mega) byte are. You learned the difference between static and dynamic memory, and that dynamic memory is not a good choice for modular computer systems.

Chapter Four

I/O Interfaces

Computer systems wouldn't be much use to us if there wasn't any way to get information in and out of them. We humans communicate with computers by using peripherals such as terminals and printers (which will be covered in more detail in later chapters). Connecting the computer to these peripherals is called **interfacing**. The computer contains boards that handle the job of interfacing the CPU and memory to the peripherals. Peripherals are often referred to as I/O (input/output) devices, and the boards that handle the interfacing job are called I/O interface boards, or just I/O boards. A typical I/O board is shown in Figure 4.1.

A single I/O interface is more commonly called an **I/O port**, or sometimes just **port** for short. One I/O board usually contains several ports, sometimes as many as eight. A port in a computer is just like a port in a country. All cargo (information) must leave and enter the country (computer) through the port. To a foreign ship (the I/O device), the port is all it ever sees of the country. The country may be different, but all ports are basically the same. However, a computer uses two different types of ports: parallel and serial.

PARALLEL AND SERIAL PORTS

In the previous chapter, you learned that a byte is a group of eight bits, and that you can represent any of

Figure 4.1 I/O board (Interfacer 4). *Courtesy of CompuPro.*

the characters in the alphabet and any punctuation mark with one byte. Since the most common I/O devices (like printers and terminals) are concerned with characters, characters are the most common type of data transferred through ports.

A **parallel port** transfers all eight bits of the byte at the same time. Each bit has its own wire to travel on. The term "parallel" comes from the fact that all the bits are transferred in parallel, or side by side.

A **serial port** transfers all eight bits of the byte one bit after another, along the same wire. One wire is used to send data from the computer to the peripheral, and another is used to send data from the peripheral to the computer.

Most peripherals are designed to be hooked up to serial ports. Some printers still use parallel ports, but most have a serial interface available as an option (there's more on this in the chapter on printers).

The RS-232C Serial Port Standard

Luckily for us, computer and peripheral manufacturers have agreed upon a basic standard interface for serial devices. The standard is called **RS-232C** and the

"RS" does not stand for "Radio Shack." It stands for "recommended standard." Most computers come with at least two RS-232C ports: one for a terminal and one for a printer.

Unfortunately, it's not as simple as it sounds. At least 8 wires are used in the "true" RS-232C interface, but data transfers can occur with as few as three wires. Many manufacturers of I/O interfaces save money by providing only three of the eight wires. These three-wire interfaces work fine in most situations, but not all. To be assured that your peripheral and computer can communicate flawlessly, and to anticipate future peripherals, we recommend that the interface you buy for your computer contain all eight wires. This may be difficult with single-board computers because you are stuck with the number of wires the manufacturer decided to give you. (And by the way, you are stuck with the number of ports too!) The record may be sounding old to you by now, but this again points out the advantage of the modular computer: you can choose true RS-232C interfaces, and you are not limited in their number.

BAUD RATES

No, **baud rate** does not refer to the pricing policies of a house of ill repute. Computers and peripherals talk to one another at some rate of speed, and they both need to be set to the same speed or one couldn't understand the other. In order to set them both to the same speed, we need some unit of measure to refer to the speed at which data is transferred. That measure is called the baud rate. Baud means **bits per second** or **BPS**. However, the number of bits transferred in one second doesn't mean much to humans. A more meaningful term is **characters per second** or **CPS**. To figure the approximate number of characters per second, divide the baud rate by ten. For example, if a terminal talks at 9600 baud, it can transmit or receive about 960 characters per second.

There are several standard baud rates at which computers and peripherals are designed to operate; these are usually selectable by a switch.

HOW MANY I/O PORTS DO I NEED?

If you are buying an all-in-one computer, you will need at least one serial port to connect to a printer (you won't need one for a terminal since the keyboard and screen are built into the computer). A parallel printer port could be acceptable, but it might limit your choice of printers, so be aware. You might want a second serial port to connect to a **modem**, which is a device that allows your computer to communicate over the phone lines. (Modems get their own chapter later.) Be careful though, not all serial ports can talk to modems without special cables, so make sure you ask.

If you are buying a computer other than an all-in-one unit, you will need at least two serial ports, one for a terminal and one for a printer. Again, a parallel port may be acceptable. Don't forget to consider a third port for a modem.

If you are buying a multi-user system, make sure there is at least one serial port per user, and one for each printer you will need. Make sure you can add more ports to accommodate future users.

A modular computer lets you add more I/O ports as you need them, for instance, when you up-grade from a single to a multi-user system.

OTHER TYPES OF INTERFACES

Terminals and printers are the most common peripherals that need to be interfaced to the computer, but there are others. Luckily, most other peripherals are designed to look like a printer or terminal to the computer, and therefore have a standard interface, such as RS-232C. However, certain special-purpose peripherals, such as floppy disk drives, require their own special interface circuitry. This is usually contained on a special-purpose I/O board. These special-purpose boards are technically I/O interfaces, but they are usually not considered to be in the same class as serial interface boards because they are not "general purpose." Rather than muddy the waters, we will treat them as special cases; for example, the disk interface will be discussed in the disk system chapter, etc.

WHAT HAVE YOU LEARNED SO FAR?

You have learned that an I/O interface or port is the place where we hook up peripherals to a computer, and that the act of hooking them up is called interfacing. You learned that the most common type of interface is the RS-232C interface, and you learned the difference between serial and parallel ports. You know to stay away from three-wire interfaces and to ask if a serial port can hook up to a modem or not. You also learned the meaning of the terms baud rate and characters per second.

Chapter Five

The Computer Enclosure

You have learned all about the insides of a computer: the CPU, memory and I/O boards. These boards make up the brain of the computer, but like our human brain they won't work too well without a head to put them in. That's where the **computer enclosure** comes in. Computer enclosures come in all shapes and sizes, and are made out of various materials. Regardless of its construction or form, the computer enclosure has one basic job: keeping the insides in. Of course some enclosures do a much better job than others. We'll see why in a moment.

The computer enclosure can be one of the most important parts of a computer system. For example, you might select the most elegant furniture for your house, but what would be the point if your roof let in the rain? Let's examine the computer enclosure in more detail.

TYPES OF ENCLOSURES

There are many different ways to build a computer enclosure; its form depends mainly on the type of computer that it is supposed to enclose. Enclosures for all-in-one computers often resemble the enclosure normally used to house a terminal. Enclosures for single-board computers can be almost any size and shape. Modular computer enclosures generally resemble a plain box.

If you are buying an all-in-one or single-board computer, you will have no choice but to use the enclosure that the manufacturer provides. The enclosure could be the deciding factor when choosing between computers with similar features. Modular computers (notably IEEE 696/S-100 computers) not only offer a selection of boards to go inside the enclosure, but offer a wide range of enclosures as well. Since most of the particulars of the enclosure for a modular computer apply to all enclosures, we'll examine that type of enclosure more closely.

The Enclosure in More Detail

Figure 5.1 shows the computer enclosure as you normally see it, with its cover securely in place. This is an enclosure for an IEEE 696/S-100 computer. Figure 5.2 is a top view of the same enclosure with its cover off.

Figure 5.1 Enclosure with cover on. *Courtesy of CompuPro.*

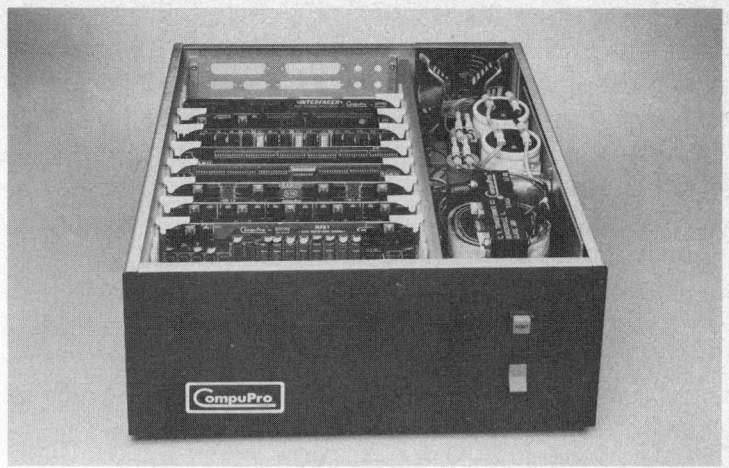

Figure 5.2 Enclosure with cover off. *Courtesy of CompuPro.*

THE POWER SUPPLY

The right side of the enclosure is taken up mostly with the **power supply**. The job of the power supply is to take the voltage that comes out of the wall and convert it into voltages that the computer boards use. It also smooths out the fluctuations in the power from the wall that normally occur. This process is called **regulating**. Some power supplies do a better job of regulating than others.

That big, boxy looking thing towards the front of the power supply is called a **transformer**. Its main job is to "transform" the high wall voltage down to a lower level for the computer. Some transformers, known as **constant voltage transformers** (or sometimes **CV transformers** for short) also provide regulation of the wall voltage. As the wall voltage fluctuates, this special kind of transformer compensates to provide stable power to the computer. Computers that don't use a constant voltage transformer in their power supply are prone to problems during "brown-outs" (when the power dips for a couple of seconds). The transformer in Figure 5.2 is a constant voltage transformer, and we recommend it highly for any serious computing.

Good power supplies should also include a **line filter**. The voltage that comes out of the wall is also known as the **line voltage**; the line filter helps to keep electrical noise on the power lines out of your computer. Noise on the line can come from a wide variety of sources such as turning on a piece of machinery, fluorescent lights, electrical storms and many more. Having a line filter keeps your computer from acting up when someone turns on a typewriter or copy machine in the next room.

THE MOTHERBOARD

To the left of the power supply is the **motherboard**. It is a long circuit board that contains many **edge connectors**. The various circuit boards, such as the CPU and memory, plug into these edge connectors. They are called "edge" connectors because they connect to the board's edge. The circuit boards that plug into the motherboard are called **daughter boards**.

The motherboard not only provides a means for holding the daughter boards in place, but also provides an electrical function as well. This brings us to the concept of a **bus**.

THE COMPUTER BUS

We normally think of a bus as a large vehicle that travels along roads and takes people from place to place. A computer bus is a series of electrical roads or pathways that takes information from place to place within the system. The motherboard contains those electrical pathways in the form of traces (the same kind that you learned were on the daughter boards to electrically connect the various ICs together). The traces on the motherboard are used to connect the various daughter boards together.

All the information in a computer travels between daughter boards on the bus. For example, if the CPU wants to send a character stored in memory to a printer, it first requests the character from the memory board. The request occurs on the bus, and the character is transferred to the CPU on the bus as well. The CPU then sends the character to the I/O board that is connected to the printer. This transfer also occurs on the bus. The I/O board then handles the transfer of the character to the printer.

Since the bus is obviously a very important part of the computer, better motherboards incorporate extra circuitry to enhance the bus' performance. This insures that all the information traveling around the computer makes it safely from one daughter board to another. The buzzwords are **termination circuitry** and **shielding**. You don't need to understand what they mean, just remember to ask if the motherboard in the computer enclosure you are thinking of buying has them or not.

The IEEE 696/S-100 Bus

In the first chapter we mentioned that the IEEE 696/S-100 bus was the most popular among modular computers, and as long as we were talking about buses, we thought it deserved another mention here. Briefly, if you buy a computer system that uses the IEEE 696/S-100 bus, you will be insured a very flexible system that can grow with you and adapt easily to your computing needs.

METAL VS. PLASTIC

While a plastic enclosure may be suitable for a "home" computer, an enclosure made out of heavy duty metal is preferred for business and industrial computing. Not only is metal more rugged and longer lasting than plastic, but it also provides an electrical shield that minimizes any interference to the computer from any other electrical or electronic equipment in the vicinity. At the same time, the metal enclosure makes the computer a "good neighbor," since it has less of a tendency to interfere with other equipment.

That is not to say that plastic doesn't have its place; most of the terminals available are housed in plastic enclosures. Some special types of plastic have a metal layer on the inside that provides almost the same shielding as a metal enclosure. The general rule is one of cost. If the item (such as terminal) is fairly inexpensive, a plastic case is acceptable. But for a mainframe that might end up costing thousands of dollars, metal is preferred.

COOLING

One of the most important jobs of the computer enclosure is to provide a means of keeping the components inside cool. The hotter a computer runs, the more likely it is to fail. Some enclosures actually do more to heat up the insides than they do to cool them! Naturally you want to avoid enclosures like that.

Most enclosures will contain a fan to force air over the boards. But just the presence of a fan does not insure good cooling. How do you tell if an enclosure is properly cooled? That's a tough one. Feel around the *outside* of the enclosure. If you notice any "hot spots," the cooling is probably inadequate. Another thing to check for is **positive pressurization** of the enclosure. Simply, this means that the fan sucks air in and blows it out the vents (see Figure 5.3). Positive pressurization is much better than **negative pressurization**, which means that air is sucked in through the vents and blown out by the fan (see Figure 5.4). One of the advantages of positive pressurization is that it allows the use of an air filter on the fan. Air filters are desirable for keeping dust and other foreign particles out of your computer. Air filters are worthless on negative

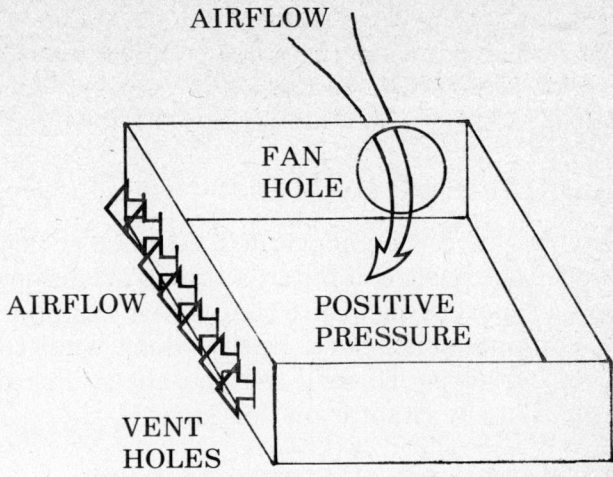

Figure 5.3 Diagram showing positive pressurization.

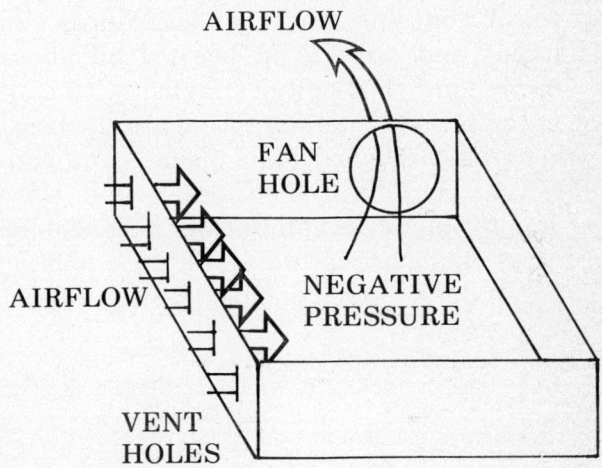

Figure 5.4 Diagram showing negative pressurization.

pressure systems because the dirty air will get sucked over all the boards and then filtered on its way out!

There is one other consideration concerning the fan, and that is how much noise it makes. It's important to pick an enclosure that has a low noise fan that *won't* whistle while you work. Recent studies have shown that most computer operator fatigue is not caused by staring at the screen, but by the constant noise of the fan.

DISK DRIVE ENCLOSURES

So far we have been concerned with the enclosures that house the basic computer, but disk drives usually come in a separate enclosure that is just as important as the computer enclosure. But we don't want to get ahead of ourselves, so we'll tell you about disk drive enclosures in the chapter on disk drives.

WHAT HAVE YOU LEARNED SO FAR?

You learned that a computer enclosure is just as important to the proper functioning of the computer as the boards it contains, and that enclosures come in many shapes and sizes. You learned all about the power supply, and that power supplies with constant voltage transformers and line filters are the best. You know what a motherboard and a bus are, and you were reminded that the IEEE 696/S-100 bus is the most popular bus for business computing. You also learned that a metal enclosure is preferable to a plastic one, and that a properly cooled enclosure (with a quiet fan) is most important.

Section 2

The Peripherals

Chapter Six

The Terminal

The **terminal** is the main communications device between you and your computer, and unless you are planning on purchasing an all-in-one computer, you will need at least one terminal. The terminal has two main elements: a TV-like screen, and a typewriter-like keyboard. A typical terminal is shown in Figure 6.1.

Figure 6.1 Televideo 910 terminal. *Courtesy of Televideo.*

A terminal may also be known as a **VDT** which stands for **video display terminal** or a **CRT** which stands for **cathode ray tube**. Cathode ray tube really describes only the screen portion of the terminal, but it has come to stand for the whole thing.

Information you type on the terminal's keyboard passes directly into the computer. The computer records this data, and then flashes it back to the screen. This happens so fast that you might think that you're typing directly on the screen, but that's not the case. What you're seeing on the screen is an "echo" of the character that you sent to the computer. Thus, when you see something that you typed on the screen, you not only know that you've typed it correctly, you also know that the computer has received it.

Since the terminal is the device that you will use most often in communicating with your computer, selection of a good terminal is very important. The electrical qualities of a terminal are important, but the terminal's "human engineering" is just as important. A fancy term for human engineering is **ergonomics**; it simply refers to the process of designing a piece of equipment so that it is easily and comfortably used by humans.

All terminals are similar in function; they let you communicate with the computer, but they can differ widely in their individual features and characteristics. Let's examine some of their features and differences.

THE SCREEN OR DISPLAY

The screen size of most terminals measures 12 inches diagonally, the same size as a small, portable TV. This screen size has proven to be the most comfortable for viewing. Some terminals will offer a slightly larger or smaller screen, but the average is 12 inches. Some all-in-one computers come with tiny 5-inch screens which, while all right for occasional viewing, can be tiring with long term use.

Displays are usually described with reference to the number of characters that they can display at one time. This number is expressed as two figures. The first is the maximum number of characters the screen can display on one line, and the second is the maximum number of lines. For example, the most common configuration is 80×24, which means that the terminal can display 80 characters per line, and 24 lines.

For general business computing use and for word processing, an 80×24 display is the minimum acceptable. All-in-one computers and "home" computers usually have much smaller displays, such as 32×16. These are totally unacceptable for business use.

Some displays are 132×24, which means they can display 132 characters per line. While these are not usually necessary for normal business computing, they can be useful for large ledger sheets.

Displays come in two main colors: black and white, and black and green. Popular in Europe, but less common in the U.S., is the black and amber display. Black and white displays have been the most predominant, but the green screen is becoming more and more popular. The black and white screen displays white characters against a black background; the black and green screen displays green characters against a black background. The green (and amber) displays are thought to be less tiring for your eyes. Note that most terminals can also display black letters on a white or green background (usually accomplished by setting a switch on the terminal). Black characters on a colored background are more pleasing to some because they resemble black characters on a typewritten page.

Another screen consideration is the glass that stands between you and the characters you see. Inexpensive terminals use standard glass that can pick up annoying reflections from the room, making the display hard to read. Better terminals use non-glare glass that minimizes reflections, but can sometimes make the display look "fuzzy." The best solution to the glare problem is a polarizing filter that minimizes the glare without sacrificing sharpness. Sometimes polarizing filters can be added as an option.

Most terminals have some kind of brightness or contrast control that will allow compensation for different light levels present in different business environments.

THE KEYBOARD

There are two main things to consider when evaluating a terminal's keyboard: the number and placement of the keys, and the "feel" of the keys. All keyboards have the basic "QWERTY" arrangement as is found on most office typewriters, but there are some things to watch out for. For example, is the Return key larger than the others, and is it well placed? How about the Tab, Backspace and Shift keys? Some terminals offer the exact same size and key placement as a standard IBM office Selectric: this can be a major comfort to a secretary new at the terminal.

Most keyboards also come with a **numeric pad**, which is usually located to the right of the keyboard and resembles a standard 10 key adding machine keyboard. This can be a real time saver if lots of numeric data must be entered into the computer.

The "feel" of the keys is much more subjective than their placement. The only way to determine whether or not you like the feel is to actually go down to your local computer store and type on the keys. If you are a touch typist, you will find the key's light touch strange at first. But you will soon adapt when you discover how fast you can fly across the keyboard when you don't have to pound it.

Detachable Keyboards

The terminal in Figure 6.1 has its display and keyboard all in one unit. The terminal in Figure 6.2 has a **detachable keyboard**. Terminals with detachable key-

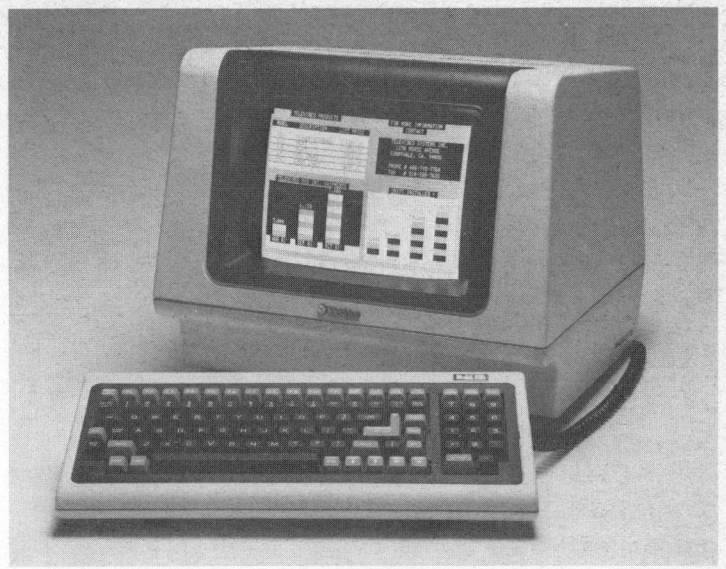

Figure 6.2 Televideo 925 terminal. *Courtesy of Televideo.*

boards tend to be a little more expensive than terminals with integrated keyboards, but they have several advantages. Taller people may find the integrated terminal uncomfortable because the display points at the neck rather than the eyes. A detachable keyboard solves this problem since the display portion can be elevated or aimed independently, while leaving the keyboard at a comfortable typing height. Many typists actually prefer to put the keyboard in their laps, which reduces strain on the shoulders.

TERMINALS AND BAUD RATES

All common terminals use an RS-232C serial interface to connect to the computer. As you learned in the chapter on I/O ports, serial devices communicate with the computer at a certain speed called the baud rate (a measure of the number of bits transferred in one second). The faster a terminal can go, the better. Most terminals are capable of communicating at 9600 baud, but better ones can communicate at 19,200 baud. It might seem odd to require a terminal to talk that fast, considering that typing 85 words a minute translates to just 70 baud. But remember that word processing programs allow us to move blocks of text around on the screen. That would be painfully slow at 70 baud, but happens in a flash at 19,200 baud.

Buying a Terminal

When you buy a terminal, the first step is to look at and type on various terminals. Be sure you buy one that you feel totally comfortable with. Make sure you can sit in a relaxed and comfortable posture at the terminal, without having to stretch your neck or type in an awkward position. Make sure you like the feel and placement of the keys. Look at the display. Is it sharp and distinct, or do the characters look fuzzy? Is the display rock solid or does it wiggle?

One final note: if you are buying the computer for someone else to use, or for more than one user, don't be afraid to take them with you when you look at terminals. Involving a person in the terminal buying decision will go a long way towards making that person feel more comfortable with the new computer, especially a first time computer user.

WHAT HAVE YOU LEARNED SO FAR?

You learned that the terminal is the primary communication device between yourself and the computer. You learned that an 80×24 display on a 12-inch screen is the most common, and that you should stay away from small screens except for occasional use. You learned that displays come in white, green and amber, and that green and amber are generally more restful on your eyes. You know that the "feel" of the keyboard and the key placement are important things to consider, as well as the fact that some keyboards are detachable. Finally, you learned that you should involve the person that will be using the terminal in the terminal buying decision.

Chapter Seven

The Printer

No matter what computer system you buy, you are going to need a printer. However, you may be surprised to find out that a good printer may end up costing you as much or more than your mainframe.

The printer is the device that provides you with a **hard copy** of the stuff that normally appears on your terminal's screen. (The display on the screen is the "soft" copy since it goes away when you turn off the computer.) Don't be fooled into thinking that you can survive without a printer. We humans are not content with looking at our data on the screen all the time. We want it on paper so we can take it with us and refer to it while using the computer for something else. Besides, most business uses of computers need a **printout** (the stuff that comes out of the printer), whether it's a sales report, an invoice, a check, correspondence, or all of the above.

There are many different types of printers, each designed to do a different job. Let's examine some of the different types of printers.

THE CONVERTED ELECTRIC TYPEWRITER

Although the converted electric typewriter may seem attractive because of its low cost, it will soon become expensive due to the high cost of keeping it running. Typewriters were not designed for heavy duty, continuous computer use, and are not recommended for serious computing applications. You need a more substantial – and reliable – printer.

THE DOT MATRIX PRINTER

The **dot matrix printer** is one of the most common types of computer printers. Dot matrix printers range from inexpensive (a few hundred dollars) to very expensive (many thousands of dollars), and they all have different features. A typical dot matrix printer is shown in Figure 7.1. One thing they all have in common is the way they form the characters they print.

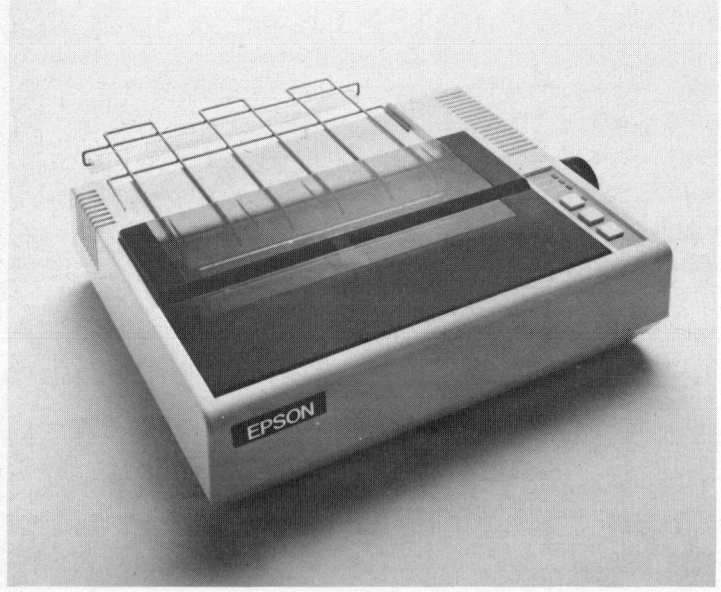

Figure 7.1 Epson MX-80 printer. *Courtesy of Epson.*

In general, a dot matrix printer uses a vertical line of pins which push out and impact paper through a ribbon. These pins are contained in the **print head**. If the print head were to remain stationary, all you would ever print is a vertical line. But the print head moves horizontally across the paper, and the printer's clever circuitry pushes out the right pins at the right times to form characters. These characters are made up of small dots caused by the pins' impact. The vertical line of pins and the horizontal movement of the print head combine to form a matrix of dots, and that's where the name "dot matrix" comes from. A series of enlarged dot matrix characters is shown in Figure 7.2.

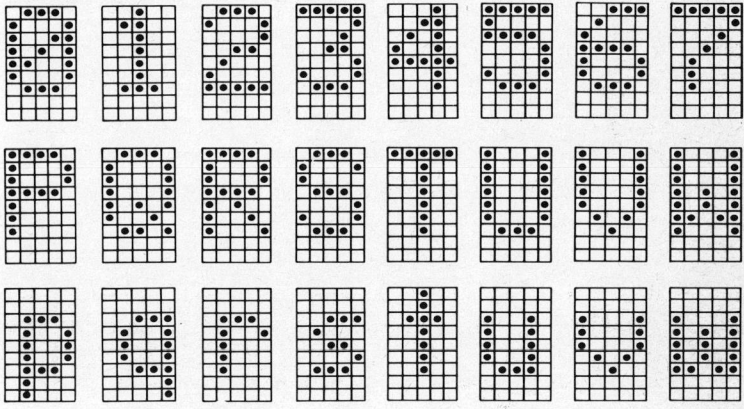

Figure 7.2 Blow up of dot matrix characters.

The less expensive the dot matrix printer, the fewer pins there are in a vertical line. That results in a smaller matrix of dots. This means that there are less dots with which to make characters, and the print quality suffers. Figure 7.3 shows an example of a printout from an inexpensive dot matrix printer. Note how the descenders of the y, g and p do not extend below the line.

Some dot matrix printers print using a technique known as **multiple pass printing**. The printer actually prints the same line two or three times, but with each pass of the print head, the paper is moved slightly.

```
   A dot matrix printer such as this
one produces descenders which do not
go below the base line of the other
letters.  Thus, the loop on a g does
not descend below the other characters
as a normal g would. Once you grow
accustomed to reading text printed on
this type of printer, you do not
notice the altered position of the
descenders.
```

Figure 7.3 Example of dot matrix printout without descenders.

This tends to fill in the spaces between the dots, making the printout much more readable. An example of a printout from a multiple pass dot matrix printer is shown in Figure 7.4 (also note how the descenders go below the line).

```
LMNOPQRSTUVWXYZ[\]^_`abcdefghijklmnopq
MNOPQRSTUVWXYZ[\]^_`abcdefghijklmnopqr
NOPQRSTUVWXYZ[\]^_`abcdefghijklmnopqrs
OPQRSTUVWXYZ[\]^_`abcdefghijklmnopqrst
PQRSTUVWXYZ[\]^_`abcdefghijklmnopqrstu
QRSTUVWXYZ[\]^_`abcdefghijklmnopqrstuv
RSTUVWXYZ[\]^_`abcdefghijklmnopqrstuvw
STUVWXYZ[\]^_`abcdefghijklmnopqrstuvwx
TUVWXYZ[\]^_`abcdefghijklmnopqrstuvwxy
UVWXYZ[\]^_`abcdefghijklmnopqrstuvwxyz
```

Figure 7.4 Example of multiple pass dot matrix printout with descenders.

One advantage of dot matrix printers is that certain models can print extremely fast. This is useful when you need to spew out huge amounts of paper in the shortest amount of time (for example, when you're billing).

The dot matrix printers discussed so far are **impact** printers because the pin actually impacts the paper (through the ribbon). Occasionally, you might hear about **electrostatic** dot matrix printers. Instead of impacting the paper, an electrical discharge actually burns the characters into a special aluminized paper. These printers should be avoided because this special paper is very costly and doesn't look so great when it's printed on (especially for checks, etc.).

THE LETTER QUALITY PRINTER

Marketing people like to call dot matrix printers **draft quality**. This means that the type quality is not the best. (Good enough to review the report yourself, but not good enough to submit to the boss.) The type quality of the **letter quality** printer is just what the name implies: good enough to send out on the company stationery. Like a conventional typewriter, the letter quality printer prints the entire character with one strike, making fully formed characters. An example of a printout from a letter quality printer is shown in Figure 7.5. Note how it compares with the type

```
A     letter     quality     printer
produces   text that is  similar
to work done on  a   typewriter.
Copies from such a printer are
less   obviously  done   on    a
computer  than  pages  printed
with   a   dot   matrix   printer.
When the  price  is comparable a
letter   quality printer is not
as    fast   as   a   dot   matrix
printer.    There is usually  a
trade  off  between  speed  and
quality.
```

Figure 7.5 Example of letter quality printout.

quality of a standard office typewriter. Of course, you don't get something for nothing. Letter quality printers are generally more expensive and slower than their dot matrix counterparts. A typical letter quality printer is shown in Figure 7.6.

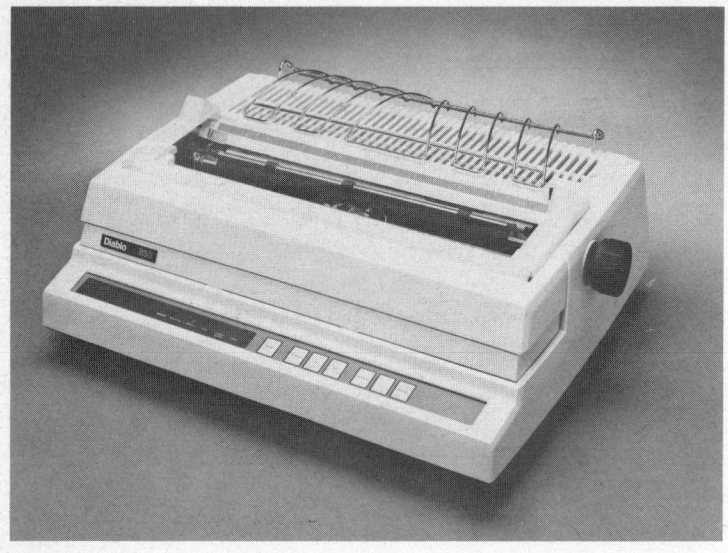

Figure 7.6 Diablo 630 letter quality printer. *Courtesy of Diablo.*

Most letter quality printers are also known as **daisy wheel** or **thimble** printers. The name "daisy wheel" comes from the fact that the various type fonts are available on small interchangeable wheels that resemble an abstract, mechanical daisy (see Figure 7.7). The "thimble" approach is shown in Figure 7.8. It is functionally quite similar to the daisy, except that all of the "petals" are bent at right angles. You can switch type fonts in a matter of seconds by changing type wheels. Most of the type wheels are made out of plastic, although some type fonts come only in a metal wheel. Some daisy wheel printers can handle both plastic and metal wheels, while others can handle only plastic.

Figure 7.7 A daisy wheel print element.

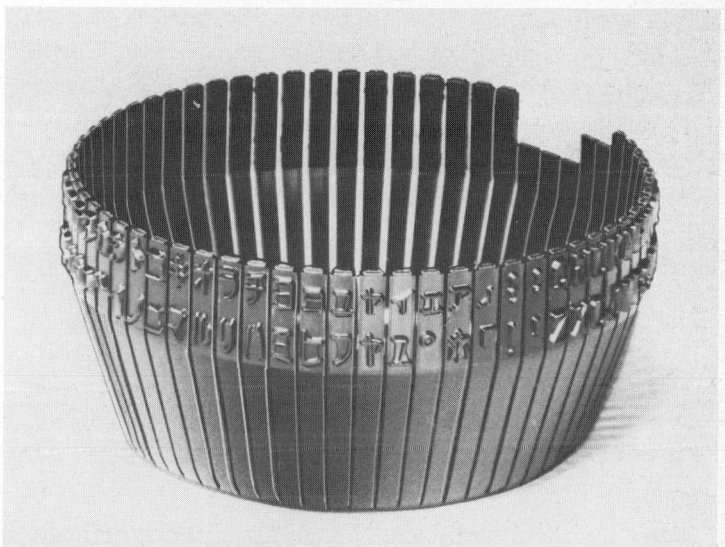

Figure 7.8 A thimble style print element. *Courtesy of NEC.*

DOT MATRIX OR LETTER QUALITY, WHICH DO I NEED?

That depends on the type of printing you need to do, and you might actually want both types: a fast dot matrix printer for billing, invoicing and check printing, and a letter quality printer for word processing. If you're on a limited budget, you might consider a multiple pass dot matrix printer until you can afford a letter quality printer. Or if you intend to do mainly word processing, but only need to print the occasional form, a letter quality printer will handle both jobs (although it will print the forms slower than a dot matrix printer).

If you're a writer, you'll definitely need a letter quality printer because editors are used to typewriters and prefer letter quality printouts over dot matrix printouts.

PRINTER ACCESSORIES

The most important accessory for any printer is paper. Most printer paper is called **fan fold** (or sometimes **z-fold**) paper. It is shown in Figure 7.9. It has little holes on either side so that the printer can handle it more easily. Each sheet is connected to the next by a perforated line. After printing out the desired number of pages, you simply tear them off along the perforation. The holes are usually on perforated strips that also tear off when you're finished printing. Once the holes have been removed, the paper becomes a standard $8\frac{1}{2}\times11$-inch sheet. Computer paper is available in white, or in alternating stripes of light green and white. The stripes are helpful when reading long rows of figures. Of course, paper manufacturers can custom make just about any kind of computer paper you want. You can even have your letterhead printed on each page.

For those who want their correspondence printed on true letterhead bond, there is the **cut sheet** or **single sheet feeder** shown in Figure 7.10. This device is used to automatically feed single sheets of paper into the printer, just as if it were fanfold paper. Fancier feeders can even feed two different sheets (the first page a letterhead and the remaining pages a matching bond) and then an envelope for the printing of a name and

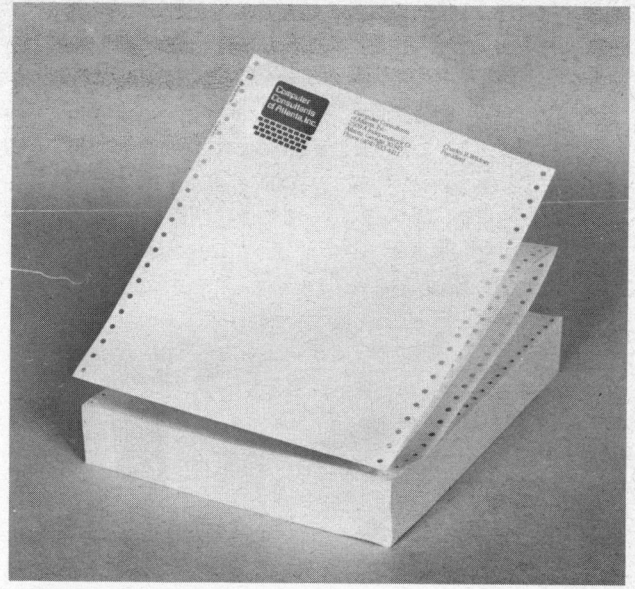

Figure 7.9 Fan-fold paper. *Courtesy of Microform.*

Figure 7.10 A cut-sheet feeder. *Courtesy of Tandy/Radio Shack.*

address. Unfortunately, these fancy single sheet feeders often cost more than the printer they're attached to, but they can be worth the investment if you do a lot of correspondence.

To facilitate the printing of continuous forms (such as checks, invoices and the like) a **forms tractor** is used (shown in Figure 7.11). It's called a tractor because the holes in the paper ride along in a belt that resembles a tractor tread. The forms tractor insures that each form is properly aligned as it goes through the printer (for example, it keeps the date from being printed in the invoice number space). Fan-fold paper is also fed through the printer on a forms tractor. The letter quality printer shown in Figure 7.6 has a forms tractor on it.

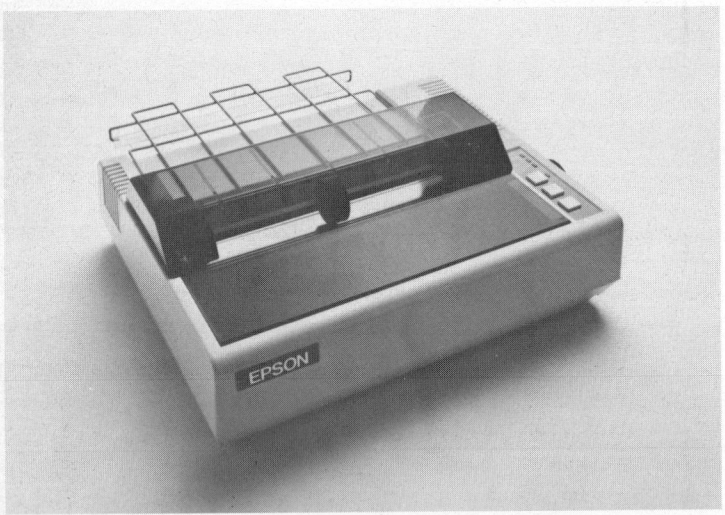

Figure 7.11 Forms tractor. *Courtesy of Epson.*

The last item on our list of printer accessories is the ribbon. Both fabric and carbon types are available, although the carbon types work only on letter quality printers (another reason why they produce such a good looking printout). Fabric ribbons are usually packaged as a continuous loop. They make pass after pass through the printer until the ink eventually dries out, giving the lowest cost per character. Carbon ribbons are good for only one pass through the printer, but they give a dark, consistent (and better looking) impression. Many people use a fabric ribbon for running drafts and intermediate printouts, and then run the final copy with a carbon ribbon.

PRINTER/TERMINALS

Most printers are output devices in that they receive data only from the computer. These are called **RO** printers; that stands for receive only. However, some printers also have keyboards, which turn them into terminals (unlike the terminals described in the previous chapter, these use paper for their display instead of the TV screen). These are called **KSR** printers, which stands for keyboard send and receive. You are probably better off with a standard terminal and an RO printer.

PARALLEL VS. SERIAL PRINTERS

Printers interface to computers in one of two ways: serial or parallel. Printers with a serial interface use the RS-232C standard. Printers with a parallel interface usually use an interface known as the **Centronics** interface. Centronics is a manufacturer of printers. The interface they designed for their printers was copied by other manufacturers, making it a de-facto standard.

Less expensive printers (such as the cheaper dot matrix types) come with a Centronics interface, but usually have a serial interface available as an option. The more expensive printers (such as a letter quality printer) usually come with a serial interface. Make sure the computer you buy has an interface to match your printer.

Generally, we prefer printers with serial interfaces because they are easier to hook up. The Centronics-style interface requires a unique kind of cable, while the serial interface uses the same cable that your terminal uses. Also, the bigger computer systems tend not to have Centronics-style printer ports. This can cause problems when you try to upgrade to a bigger system and want to keep your existing printer.

PRINTER SPEEDS VS. BAUD RATES

The difference between the speed at which the computer talks to the printer and the speed at which the printer prints can be confusing. The baud rate (the speed at which the computer talks to the printer) is usually not the same as the rate at which the characters can be printed. The printer can usually accept a character from the computer much faster than it can print it. However, the computer must wait until the character has been printed until it can send another.

Most printers use a small amount of memory called a **buffer** to stack up characters waiting to be printed. The computer might send a whole page-full of characters to the printer at a very high speed and then wait until the printer's buffer is empty (meaning all the characters have been printed) before sending more.

If the printer is being used with a single-user system, there is not much reason for sending all those characters at high speed just to wait around to send some more. But if the printer is being used with a multi-user system, the computer can do work for someone else while the printer is printing the characters in its buffer.

WHAT HAVE YOU LEARNED SO FAR?

You learned that you will need a printer, and that a good one can cost as much as the mainframe. You learned that dot matrix printers can print fast, but their printout doesn't look as nice as the printout from a letter quality printer. You learned about daisy wheels and a variety of printer accessories. You learned that you might need both a letter quality and a dot matrix printer to handle different printing chores. Finally, you now know to stay away from converted electric typewriters and electrostatic printers.

Chapter Eight

The Mass Storage System

The **mass storage system** is the place in the computer system where information (data and programs) is stored for later use. It is a form of memory, but is not the same as the computer's RAM (Random Access Memory). In the chapter about memory, you learned that a computer's RAM is used by the computer in its moment to moment operation. In other words, programs and data that are currently being used by the computer are stored in its RAM. In contrast, programs and data that are not currently being used are stored in the mass storage system. It's like the filing system found in most offices. All of a customer's data is stored in a file folder, which is usually kept in the filing cabinet. When you want to look at the data in that customer's file, you get the file from the cabinet and put it on your desk to use. When you are done, you file the information in the cabinet again. You can't use the data while it's in the filing cabinet, you must get the file and put it on your desk, first.

The mass storage system of a computer has the same function as your office filing system. It provides a convenient place to store programs and data that you aren't currently using. (In fact, once stored, the data and programs are called **files**.) Your desk is similar to the computer's RAM; you must put the information on the desk (into RAM) before you can use it. When you're done, you must put the information away for future use.

One of the reasons that computers need mass storage systems is that the amount of storage area (or **capacity**) of a mass storage system is usually much greater than the amount of RAM in a computer. A typical computer for a medium-sized office may have only 128K bytes of RAM, but it may have 2.4 *mega*-bytes of mass storage. Another reason for using mass storage is that a computer's RAM is **volatile**, which means that the data goes away when the power is turned off. On the other hand, mass storage is **non-volatile**, which means that the information is retained when you turn off the computer.

TYPES OF MASS STORAGE SYSTEMS

The earliest type of mass storage used was **magnetic tape**. These are the refrigerator-size units with the big reels that you always see in movies whenever they show a computer (it's either the big reels or the big board of flashing lights). The unit that holds the tape reels is called the **tape drive**; they are still in wide use today (see Figure 8.1). A single tape drive is capable of holding massive amounts of information, costs quite a lot, and takes up a lot of space. They are found only on big computer installations and are not used in the typical small business computer application.

The process of storing data on the tape is much the same as that used by home audio and video tape recorders. When microcomputers first appeared, the portable cassette recorder was used as an inexpensive way to save programs and data. Some personal computers still use the cassette recorder for this purpose. However, for serious computing, the cassette recorder should not even be considered. You need a faster and more reliable form of storage.

Figure 8.1 Tape drive. *Courtesy of DEC.*

That brings us to the floppy disk system. Figure 8.2 shows a **floppy disk drive** with a **floppy diskette** next to it. The floppy disk is the most commonly used mass storage device in small business computers. The floppy diskette (or just **diskette** for short) is what actually contains the stored information. The diskette is a thin piece of mylar (a type of plastic) that is coated with magnetic particles just like audio or video tape. This mylar is disk-shaped and is protected by a paper jacket. An exploded view of a floppy diskette is shown in Figure 8.3.

A **hard disk system** works in much the same way as a floppy disk system, except that the diskette is rigid

Figure 8.2 8″ floppy disk drive (out of the cabinet), with diskette. *Courtesy of Shugart.*

rather than floppy. The diskette (called a **platter** in hard disk systems) is usually made out of aluminum and is coated with the same magnetic particles used on floppy diskettes. Hard disk systems are capable of storing much more information than floppy disk systems, but also cost much more. A hard disk drive is shown in Figure 8.4.

Cartridge tape systems are similar in concept to the large tape drives we discussed earlier, but are much smaller in both size and cost. A picture of a cartridge tape drive is shown in Figure 8.5. Don't confuse cartridge tape systems with cassette tapes; they're not the same. Cartridge tape systems are not used as the main storage system of a computer, but are used

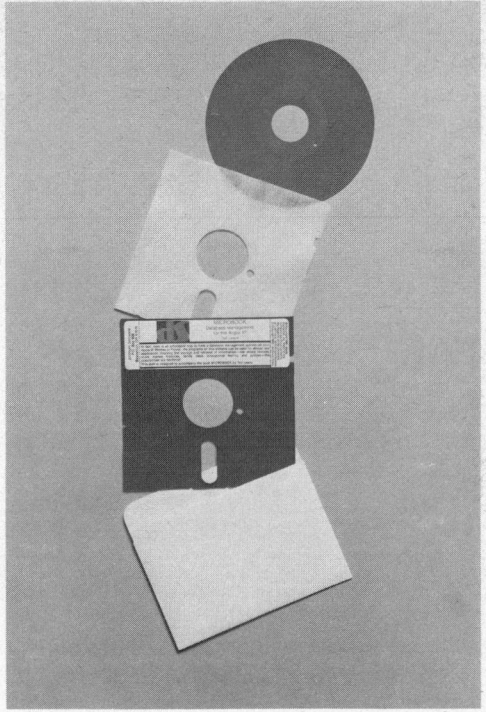

Figure 8.3 Exploded view of a floppy diskette.

mainly for keeping **backup** copies of important data. The term backup refers to a second copy of the data that is kept in case the original is destroyed or lost.

That's a quick overview of the different types of mass storage systems, now let's examine them in more detail.

THE FLOPPY DISK SYSTEM

As we mentioned earlier, the floppy disk system is the most common form of mass storage in use today. The floppy disk system is made up of four different parts:

The floppy diskette: The floppy diskette is the part of the system that actually retains the information. It

Figure 8.4 Hard disk drive (out of the cabinet).
*Courtesy of **Shugart**.*

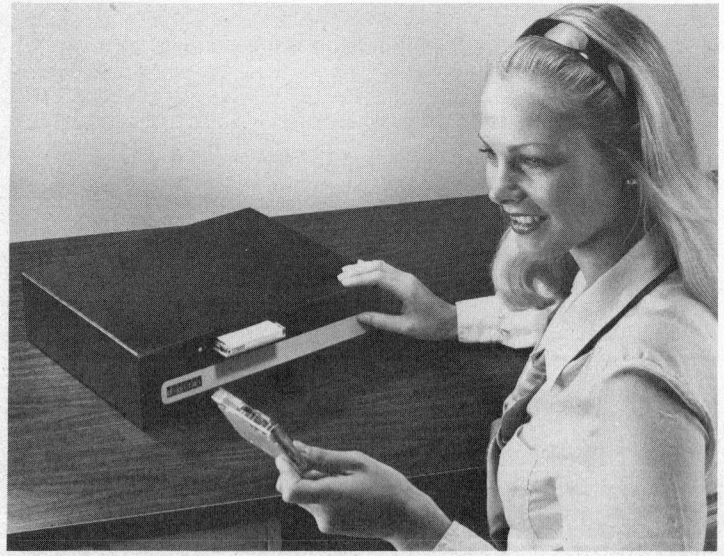

Figure 8.5 Cartridge tape drive. *Courtesy of DEC.*

is a thin piece of disk-shaped mylar that rotates inside a paper jacket. Floppy diskettes come in two sizes: 5¼-inch and 8-inch. The 8-inch size is the standard size; the 5¼-inch size is known as a **mini-floppy**. Using the diskette simply involves inserting it into the disk drive and removing it when your computing session is over or when you wish to change over to another diskette.

The disk drive(s): The disk drive is the mechanism that holds the diskette and causes it to rotate. It is also responsible for getting data onto the diskette (called **writing**) and off the diskette (called **reading**). Disk drives come in both 8 and 5¼-inch sizes.

The disk drive enclosure: The disk drive enclosure is the box that holds the disk drives and a power supply for them (see Figure 8.6). Since the disk drives generate a substantial amount of heat, the cooling of

Figure 8.6 Dual floppy disk drive enclosure.
Courtesy of CompuPro.

the disk drive enclosure is important. The heat can damage the floppy diskettes and the drives themselves. See Chapter Five, The Computer Enclosure, for a discussion of what makes a good enclosure; all those concepts apply to the disk drive enclosure as well. It is most important that the disk drive enclosure have positive pressurization, which means that air is sucked in through the fan and blown out through vents in the enclosure. This is especially important because the dust in the air is trapped in a filter before the air is circulated around the disk drives. If the air is sucked in through the vents and blown out through the fan (called negative pressurization) the sensitive disk drives and diskettes will be used as the filter. This can be fatal to your data! For a more complete discussion of positive and negative pressurization, refer to Chapter Five.

The disk controller board: This is a special kind of I/O board that plugs into the mainframe's motherboard. Its job is to handle the flow of data to and from the computer's RAM and the disk drives.

These are the basic parts of any floppy disk system. Now let's examine some of the differences between the various floppy disk systems.

8-Inch or 5¼-Inch – Which Do I Want?

Size is the most obvious difference between floppy disk systems. The 5¼-inch systems are cute and inexpensive. They are probably satisfactory for personal computers, but they generally don't have enough capacity (hold enough characters) for serious business computing. Systems that use 8-inch drives hold significantly more information. Another advantage of 8-inch systems is that a standard exists for the way data is stored on the 8-inch diskette. (It was developed by IBM.) This insures that a diskette written on one system may be read by another. The 8-inch IBM format is a standard format which software manufacturers use for the programs they distribute.

You want an 8-inch floppy disk system.

How Much Capacity Are You Talking About?

The capacity of a floppy disk system (or all mass storage systems for that matter) is measured by the number of bytes or characters it can hold. A typical 8-inch floppy disk system with two drives can store up to 2.4 megabytes (2.4 million characters). Most dual drive 5¼-inch systems store only about 250K bytes (a quarter of a million characters), which is a lot less than an 8-inch system can store.

Single or Double Density and Single or Double-Sided

You have probably seen these terms bandied about in the sales literature. Confused? Here are the answers:

When floppy disk drives first appeared, they were **single density** devices (but no one knew it because double density didn't exist yet). Single density drives stored a lot of data, but there is always the demand to store more data. This demand led to the development of **double density** disk drives. These allowed twice as much data to be stored in the same space, hence the name double density.

Double density didn't satisfy everyone; more storage was still needed. Why not write on both sides of the diskette? That's what **double-sided** drives do. This effectively doubles the storage capacity. Double density combined with double-sided is sometimes referred to as **quad-density**.

You may hear the term **dual density**. This is not the same as double density. Dual density means that the floppy disk system can handle both single and double density diskettes.

Can I Get By with One Floppy Disk Drive?

No. Copying data from one diskette to another with only one drive is a pain in the neck. Some software *re-*

quires the use of two drives (one for programs, the other for data). The money you might save by buying only one drive will quickly be lost in the time spent just making backup copies of data. Take our advice and buy two drives to start with.

HARD DISK SYSTEMS

The hard disk is used when the capacity of a floppy disk system is not enough. A small hard disk can store about 5 megabytes – twice as much as a dual 8-inch floppy system. A large hard disk might store more than 100 megabytes! Note that hard disks are usually not used to replace floppies, but are used in addition to them. The hard disk's platter is the part that actually holds the data. It normally stays inside the drive at all times; it is **non-removable**. **Removable media** (the media is the platter) hard disks are now becoming available and will be more popular in the future.

Hard disk systems initially cost a lot more than floppy disk systems, but the cost-per-byte stored may actually be less. The hard disk system consists of the same basic parts as the floppy disk system:

The hard disk drive: The mechanism that holds the platter and is responsible for getting the data on and off it.

The drive enclosure: The box that holds the disk drive and its power supply. Proper cooling is extremely important in a hard disk enclosure because hard disks generate a lot more heat than floppy disks.

The hard disk controller: The board that plugs into the mainframe's motherboard that is responsible for handling the flow of data to and from the computer's RAM and the hard disk.

HOW MUCH MASS STORAGE DO I NEED?

That is determined mainly by what it is that you want to do with your computer. The best bet is to discuss this topic with your computer salesperson. Just make sure that you are honest about the number of items in your inventory, etc. At the very least, you will want a dual 8-inch disk drive system that is capable of dual density operation. Again, this points out the advantages of the modular computer system — more storage capacity may be added as your needs grow (and they will!).

WHAT HAVE YOU LEARNED SO FAR?

You learned why you want to have a mass storage system on your computer, and what kinds of mass storage systems are available. You learned that the 8-inch floppy disk system is the most desirable, and to stay away from cassettes and 5¼-inch drives for serious business use. You learned the difference between single and double density, and single and double-sided. You also learned that you can't get along with only one drive. You know what a hard disk system is, and what the difference is between it and a floppy disk system. You know that the amount of storage you require is dependent on what you're doing with your computer. You learned to ask your computer salesperson for help in determining your storage requirements.

Chapter Nine

The Modem

Talking to your computer (or having your computer talk to other computers) over the telephone lines is becoming more popular every day. Applications range from community bulletin boards to transferring data between your branch offices and tying into information utilities. The device that allows your computer to send and receive informaton over the phone lines is called a **modem** (short for modulator/demodulator). It translates computer data into tones, which may then be sent and received over the phone lines. Some modems talk at relatively slow speeds (about 30 characters per second) while fancier modems can communicate at over 200 characters per second. Of course, the faster they go the more expensive they are.

Modems were invented back in the days when it was far too expensive for each executive or small office to have its own computer. Modems allowed a terminal to be connected to a big computer over the phone lines. The big computer was usually owned by a big company; the smaller company just bought time on the big computer. Many users were able to call the big computer and share it at the same time. That's where the term **time-sharing** comes from.

Modems are still used to access large computers, but many people now use them to call their own small computer. For example, suppose you were away from the office on a business trip and you wanted to check something on the computer back at the office. If your computer at the office has a modem connected to it, all you would need to call your computer from your hotel room is a terminal and another modem.

It is also very useful to have your small computer call up and access a larger computer, and to use some of your computer's smarts to take the workload off you. For example, suppose you are tied into an information utility that offers a news service. You might have your computer call at regular intervals, scan for stories that are of interest to you, and store them in your own computer system. You could then examine them at your convenience. This could save you hours of time scanning through the articles yourself.

As you can see, the seemingly simple modem has a myriad of uses. Let's examine modems in more detail:

THE ACOUSTICALLY COUPLED MODEM

The most common and inexpensive type of modem is the **acoustically coupled** modem (sometimes called an **acoustic coupler**). It is acoustically coupled because you place the telephone handset right on top of the modem; the microphone and speaker in the handset fit into special rubber cups (see Figure 9.1). Tones come out of a little speaker that sits right next to the handset's mouthpiece. Tones coming out of the handset's earphone are picked up by a microphone in the modem.

These modems are limited to about 300 baud (remember that baud is another term for bits per second) because of the limitations of the telephone's handset. All of these modems use a standard set of tones for conveying the information. These tones were chosen by Ma Bell, and are called Bell 103. All acoustically coupled modems use Bell 103; this allows them to talk to any other modem.

Figure 9.1 Acoustic-coupled modem. *Courtesy of Novation, Inc.*

DIRECT CONNECT MODEMS

In order to send data over the phone lines faster, it is necessary to bypass the telephone handset. As the name implies, this is what a **direct connect** modem does. This type of modem connects directly to the phone lines, bypassing not only the handset, but the whole telephone. Besides being able to talk at much higher baud rates, the direct connect modem allows several other features to be incorporated. Some have the ability to answer the phone line if it rings (called **auto-answer**) and connect the line through to the computer (through the modem of course). Some can also dial out (called **auto-dial**), allowing automatic calling of another computer (at night, for example, when the rates are lower). A picture of a direct connect modem is shown in Figure 9.2.

Direct connect modems usually communicate at 1200 baud using a different standard set of tones than Bell 103. The 1200 baud standard is called Bell 212. A Bell 103 modem cannot talk to a Bell 212 modem. Bell 212 modems generally cost three to four times more than a Bell 103 modem.

Figure 9.2 Direct-connect modem. *Courtesy of Novation, Inc.*

Some Bell 103 modems are also direct connect, thereby avoiding some of the disadvantages of the acoustic coupler (like stray noise affecting the data) and gaining some advantages like auto-answer and auto-dial. Also, some direct connect modems can operate at 300 or 1200 baud using either the Bell 103 or 212 standards.

ORIGINATE AND ANSWER MODE MODEMS

The modem that originates the phone call is called an **originate mode** modem. The modem that answers the call on the other end is called an **answer mode** modem. Some modems are capable of both originating and answering a call (but not at the same time). These are called **originate/answer mode** modems. Most acoustically coupled modems are originate mode devices, and are often referred to as *originate only* modems.

HOW DO I HOOK UP A MODEM TO MY COMPUTER?

Most modems use the RS-232C interface, so they should plug into your computer just as if they were a terminal or printer. However, there is a slight snag. Remember that modems were designed to plug directly into terminals, not computers. What that means is this: The modem is trying to send data to the computer on one wire (we'll call it wire A), and receive data from the computer on another wire (we'll call it wire B). But the computer is also trying to send data on wire A and receive data on wire B. This won't work, since the data can't be bumping into one another (it's kind of like driving the wrong way on a one way street). So if you try to plug a modem into a port designed to accept a terminal or printer, all the connections will be reversed (but only at one end). The wires are in the wrong place for plugging into a computer. This can be corrected inside the computer (better RS-232C interfaces have a provision to reverse the connections) or by a special cable known as a **null modem cable**. This cable reverses the connections at one end, and your guess is as good as ours as to why it's called a null modem cable. Don't try and use a null modem cable to hook up a printer or terminal.

Some modems are designed to plug directly into the mainframe's motherboard. They don't use an RS-232C port at all, thereby avoiding the cable problem. They may also offer other advantages, such as actually being able to control more of the computer's functions remotely. These are of the direct connect type (because they usually include such features as auto-dial and auto-answer) and can be Bell 103 or 212 compatible. (Don't be confused—these are direct connect modems because they "direct connect" to the phone lines, not the computer.)

USING A MODEM WITH A TERMINAL

As mentioned earlier, modems were originally designed to allow terminals to connect to a computer over long distances; they can still be used that way. The modem plugs into the back of the terminal and the phone goes in the acoustic coupler. Dial up the computer and you're in business. If you want to talk to your own computer, it will have to be equipped with an answer mode modem. If you want to talk to an information utility (such as The Source), you dial their computer instead. Your own computer would not be needed in this instance; all you would need is a terminal, a modem and a telephone.

WHAT HAVE YOU LEARNED SO FAR?

You learned that a modem is a device that is used to send data over the phone lines using tones. There are two standard sets of tones: Bell 103 for low speed communication, and Bell 212 for high speed communication. You learned the difference between an acoustically coupled and direct connect modem, and the difference between originate and answer modes. You know that modems connect to terminals or computers using the RS-232C interface, and that some computers will require the use of a null modem cable. Finally, you learned that modems are useful for a number of applications.

Section 3

Software

One of the most important parts of any computer system is the **software**, a term used to refer to all the various **programs** that are used in a computer system. Software is like a road map for the computer; it instructs the computer what to do with the data you enter from the keyboard, how to send it out to the printer and how to perform all those wonderful tricks you bought a computer for in the first place.

Without software, a computer is just a bunch of electronic gizmos that won't do anything at all. Computer hardware by itself has no personality; this is determined by the software. Word processing software turns the computer into a word processor, accounting software turns the computer into an accounting tool, and game software allows you to blast Klingons to the other side of the galaxy.

The next two chapters will introduce you to software.

Chapter Ten

The Operating System

Your computer will require two types of software: The first type is the **operating system**, sometimes called the **OS** (say "oh ess") for short. The operating system is the traffic cop of the computer system. It directs the flow of data around the computer system (to and from memory, mass storage, printers, terminals, modems, etc.) just as a traffic cop directs the flow of cars in a busy intersection. The operating system also allows you to perform some elementary tricks, such as copying something from one diskette to another.

Every computer has an operating system of some sort. The operating system is not the personality of the computer, but it is what you use to tell the computer which personality to assume. The operating system knows how to get data on and off the disk drives, and how to get data from the terminal. When you tell the operating system to get the word processing personality from the diskette, you do so by typing a **command** on the keyboard. The operating system would then get the word processing program from the diskette, put it into the computer's RAM and cause the program to come to life. Voila! Your computer is now a word processor.

The operating system will usually seem to vanish while you are word processing, but it's actually still around waiting to do work for the word processing program. When the word processor needs to send your memo to the printer, it will not talk to the printer itself. Instead, it will give the characters to the operating system and the operating system will send the characters to the printer. When the word processor wants to save that memo on diskette for future reference, it does not save the memo itself, it asks the operating system to do the work.

Why go to all that trouble? Because like the RS-232C standard that allows all terminals to hook up to computers in a standard way, the majority of small business computers use a "standard" operating system. That operating system is called **CP/M** (more about CP/M in a bit). The advantage of the standard operating system is that all word processing programs, accounting packages, etc., talk to the operating system in the same way. The word processing package doesn't have to know any of the details of your computer system, like what kind of disk drives you have. This allows one software package to work on a wide variety of different computers.

THE CP/M OPERATING SYSTEM

By far the most popular operating system is CP/M from Digital Research. CP/M stands for "Control Program for Microcomputers." CP/M is available for both 8 and 16 bit computers. You definitely want to have a computer that uses the CP/M operating system. Most of the software available for small business computers is written for the CP/M operating system. Without CP/M, you're going to have big trouble finding software to use with your computer.

Although CP/M was developed by Digital Research, you don't have to buy it from them. CP/M is usually included with the basic computer system; it is provided by the manufacturer of that system. That's so CP/M can be tailored to that particular computer system, and the manufacturer is usually the best at doing that.

CP/M is a **single-user operating system** which means that it is intended for use by one person at a time. For multi-user systems where more than one person can use the computer at a time, you need a **multi-user operating system**. There is a multi-user version of CP/M called **MP/M**. MP/M is also available for both 8 and 16 bit processors.

OTHER OPERATING SYSTEMS

As far as single-user operating systems go, CP/M dominates the small business computer market. There are a few CP/M look-alikes, but we recommend you stick with real CP/M. When you've got the real thing, you don't have to worry about what programs may or may not work with the look-alike (because sometimes they actually don't look so much alike!).

In the multi-user operating system arena, MP/M has a few contenders. **OASIS** is a multi-user operating system from Phase One that has enjoyed some popularity, especially in Europe, but it has one major drawback. You can't use CP/M programs with it. Like MP/M, OASIS is available for both 8 and 16 bit processors; however the 8 bit version runs only on Z-80 based computers.

UNIX and all UNIX look-alikes have caused quite a stir recently. It is being touted as *the* system by many industry sooth-sayers. UNIX is popular amongst the academic community, but it doesn't really have much to offer the business computer user. Our opinion is that UNIX will not be widely used in the small business computing environment for a whole flock of reasons (no compatible applications software is just one reason), but we could be wrong. Only time will tell. UNIX is available only for 16 bit computers.

WHAT HAVE YOU LEARNED SO FAR?

You learned that every computer needs some type of operating system, and that most small business computers use the CP/M operating system. You learned that the operating system is the traffic cop of the computer system, directing the flow of data around the system. You know that the operating system is not the personality of the computer, but is used to tell the computer which personality to assume. You learned that other software uses the operating system to move data about in the system. You learned that there are both single and multi-user operating systems available. Finally, you learned that you definitely want a computer that uses the CP/M operating system so that you will have a large amount of business-oriented software from which to choose.

Chapter Eleven

Applications Software

In the previous chapter, you learned that the operating system software is not the personality of your computer, but is used to tell the computer which personality to assume. The **applications program** is what gives your computer a personality. Examples of applications software include word processing programs, accounting programs, financial modeling and forecasting programs, mailing list programs and a Star Trek game program. What makes the computer such a powerful tool is its ability to assume any of these personalities and more, simply by using the appropriate applications software. After all, it was the application of a computer that got you interested in the first place, right?

This chapter will give you a quick overview of some of the more popular types of applications software.

WORD PROCESSING

One of the most common uses of a small business computer is as a replacement for the electric typewriter. That's what a word processing program does, although the big advantage of a word processor is that it replaces the typewriter *and* hundreds of bottles of correction fluid. Most people who are accustomed to using typewriters may find word processing a little bewildering at first, but after a few hours most won't ever want to return to the typewriter. This entire book was written using an IEEE 696/S-100 bus computer system and a word processing program.

Sometimes a word processor is called a **text editor**. Text editors don't usually have as many features or capabilities as a word processor. It's kind of like the difference between a blender and a food processor. But notice that we said "usually." That's because it's up to the manufacturer to call their product a word processor or a text editor, but *usually* word processors do more.

When using a word processor, all typing is done at a terminal. The characters appear on the screen exactly as they will when they are printed. Corrections are done magically. Whole words and sentences appear and disappear with a few keystrokes. Whole paragraphs and pages can be moved about at will. Adding new words, sentences, or pages can be done effortlessly. When the document is exactly right, then it can be sent to the printer. If you need another original, you can print it again. If you don't like the margins, you can change them and print it again, all in a flash. These are just some of the magical things a good word processing program can do.

Some word processors have the ability to take a form letter and print multiple copies of it, but each addressed to a different person. This is called **mail-merging**, because the names and addresses from a mailing list are successively merged into the letters. This is quite useful if you do a lot of direct mail advertising and/or sales.

Things to look for when shopping for a word processing package: How easy is it to use? Are the most common commands well thought out? Will it "help" you if you forget a command? Do you see the text on the screen exactly as it will be printed (including showing you where the page ends), or do you have to go through some complicated procedure to "print" the document on the screen first? Can documents be printed easily? Most importantly, can it use the terminal and printer you like?

Spelling Checkers

A popular addition to a word processing program is the **spelling checker**. These programs take a document and actually proofread it in a matter of seconds. It does this by comparing all the words in a document to the words stored in the spelling checker's dictionary. These dictionaries usually contain over 20,000 words.

When a spelling checker is finished comparing all the words in its dictionary to the words in your document, it will show you (usually one by one) all the words that it thinks are misspelled. Two types of words will show up in this list: those that are spelled incorrectly, and those that are not contained in the dictionary. Words that are not in the dictionary may then be added to it for future use. Words that are misspelled are marked with a special character in the original document, then the word processor is invoked to find the special marks and correct the words.

Things to look for when shopping for a spelling checker are its ease of use, speed of operation, and size of the dictionary. They all check spelling, but how easy is it to add a word to the dictionary? Or delete one? Some proofread quite quickly, some are painfully slow. The size of the dictionary is usually the least important factor, as long as it contains at least 20,000 words. Some spelling checkers offer special-purpose dictionaries such as legal and medical dictionaries.

Several word processing packages include an optional spelling checker. The quality of the spelling checker may not always be the same as the word processor, but any general-purpose spelling checker may be used with most word processors.

THE ELECTRONIC SPREADSHEET

The **electronic spreadsheet** or **spreadsheet simulator** is one of the most useful pieces of software ever developed. It allows easy manipulation of numerical data for financial planning and forecasting, inventory control and any other task that requires a series of calculations.

The electronic spreadsheet uses the terminal's screen as a window to a large, imaginary sheet of paper. The paper is divided into rows and columns, just like standard ledger paper. The intersection of a row and column is called a **cell.** Rows are designated with numbers, and columns are designated with letters. A cell is designated by the combination of the row number and column letter that intersect it. For example, cell A5 is the intersection of column A and row 5.

A cell can contain a number like 234, or a formula like A2+A3, which means "the contents of cell A2 plus the contents of cell A3." If cell A2 contained the number 12 and cell A3 contained the number 13, and cell A5 contained the formula A2+A3, the screen would show 12 in A2, 13 in A3 and 25 in A5 (the sum of A2 and A3). Now comes the magic. If you change the contents of cell A2 to 15, cell A5 will immediately show 28 (15+13). A cell can also contain text, like the word "TOTAL," so the spreadsheet is easily read.

The electronic spreadsheet is useful for an unlimited array of tasks. The most immediately obvious use is financial forecasting and modeling. You can play "what if" games with your company's sales, budget, income, costs, overhead, etc., either separately or all at the same time! When your "fine tuning" is complete, you can print out a copy of the spreadsheet to show the boss (or your staff). This application alone is worth the price of admission, but there are many more things you can do with a spreadsheet simulator.

THE DATABASE MANAGEMENT SYSTEM

Any collection of data, or more usually groups of data, is called a **database**. For example, all the names, addresses and phone numbers of your customers would be a database. Wouldn't it be nice to have all this information stored in the computer system and be able to retrieve it at will? Well, that's exactly the function of a **database management system**, sometimes abbreviated **DBMS**. It manages a database, in this case your clients' names, addresses and phone numbers.

Let's say you have more than just your customers' name, address and phone number stored. Suppose you also have a record of every item that a client purchased from you in the past, the type of items that they usually buy, and how much money they spend on the average purchase. Here's where the power of the database manager comes in. You can ask the database manager to print you a list of all the customers that live in your state, have purchased an item worth over $100 in the last 6 months, make an average purchase of $50 or more, and have bought some specific item in the past. The database manager will happily print the list. Say an item has been recalled by the manufacturer; you can have the database manager print a list of all the customers that ever bought that item.

The type of database manager that allows sorting through all this data looking only for those items that meet certain criteria is called a **relational database management system**.

A powerful database manager, properly applied, can be a great asset to any business. The uses are limitless. But there is a "gotcha" when dealing with database managers. Database management systems are not usually designed for the non-computer type (like you) to use. What this means is that you can't buy a database management system and expect to start using it like you would use a word processor. It will usually require a programmer to write a program to make the database manager easier for you to use, but we're getting ahead of ourselves here. This topic will be discussed later. We brought up the subject of databases because we wanted you to get a flavor for the types of problems such a system could solve.

ACCOUNTING PACKAGES

Accounting is one of the most sought after uses of a small business computer. A good accounting package can contain the general ledger, accounts payable, accounts receivable, and payroll functions. Sometimes these are sold as separate progams, but they should all be able to talk to one another. For example, if a check comes in on a customer's account, the person operating the computer would "post" it using the accounts receivable function, but the general ledger should be automatically informed that a check has been deposited. The accounts payable and payroll functions should then know whether or not there is enough money to write checks.

The only way to select a good accounting package is to have your accountant help you. Sometimes you won't be able to find one that suits your needs, or fits in with the way you've been doing it for years by hand. That brings us to the next topic of discussion: software customization.

CUSTOM VERSUS CANNED SOFTWARE

Sometimes you can walk into your computer dealer and buy a piece of software off-the-shelf and it will do just what you want. You might have to evaluate similar products from different manufacturers to find one you like, but once you find it, you can use it as it comes. A word processor or spelling checker is a good example of a program that is used just as purchased. That type of software is called **canned software**.

It is not very likely that you will be able to find a canned accounting package that does everything the way you want it, but sometimes you can adapt your way of doing things to the way the program would rather have them done. Doing this can save you lots of money. However, most people will find that they want a package **customized** to their specific needs. The usual procedure is to find a package that is close to what you want, and then have it modified by a professional programmer (who should be on the staff at the place where you buy your computer). The last resort is to have a software package written for you "from the ground up." This can get quite expensive, but may be worth the cost if you need something really special.

Earlier, in our discussion of database managers, we talked about having a program customized to make it easier for non-computer types to use. The database manager contains commands that allow you to search the database with various criteria, updating the data, etc. These commands are usually designed with the programmer in mind, not you. However, a program can be written which speaks your language on one side, and the database's language on the other. Its job is to provide you with easy-to-use commands and to convert them into the complex commands that the database manager understands. This type of program is called a **shell** because it forms a shell around the database manager, making it easier to use. Having a custom shell written for a standard program (such as a database manager) is a very common example of customizing a piece of canned software.

"USER-FRIENDLY" SOFTWARE

Almost everything having to do with computers these days is advertised as being **user-friendly**. What this means is that the computer will treat you (the user) in a friendly fashion if you make a mistake or forget what to do next. Printing a cute error message as your data is lost forever is *not* our idea of being user-friendly. Giving you a chance to save all that data *before* it gets lost forever is user-friendly.

There really is no such thing as user-friendly hardware. It's the software that's user-friendly. Most of the better software available contains a "help" function that guides you through troublesome spots. User-friendliness in a piece of software is a good thing to have.

Be aware of one point: Sometimes user-friendly software can be a double-edged sword: useful before you are familiar with a program, but tedious and even annoying once you get used to the way the program operates. Make sure that you can reduce the level of friendliness. Just like real friends, seeing too much of them can make them enemies.

GAMES

No computer would seem complete unless it also played a few games. Some computers are designed to play games quite well (with fancy color graphics and joystick controllers). But computers designed for business use are not optimized for game playing. There are some pretty impressive games available for them, however.

Most people equate computer games with the video games you see in the local arcade: Space Invaders, Asteroids, etc. These highly visual games are best played on a computer better suited to game playing (such as an ATARI computer). If you really want to play these types of computer games, get yourself another computer for playing them. They don't cost very much, and can be a lot of fun.

The type of games for which business computers are best suited are text-oriented games. These are games where the play consists mainly of interacting with the computer through words and sentences. Star Trek was one of the first text-oriented computer games. It puts you at the helm of the Enterprise (you're Captain Kirk) and Spock, Scotty, Uhura and the rest (including the attacking Klingon ships) are played by the computer. Another popular type of game is the Adventure type of game. In the original version, you explore a giant cave with hundreds of rooms looking for treasure, dealing with the various inhabitants of the cave, all the while trying to solve the cave's mysteries. Other versions based on the Adventure idea have appeared, such as solving a baffling murder mystery — you're the famous sleuth wandering through a giant mansion. No rules are given for these games; half of the game is figuring out the rules. It's an Adventure, after all!

Most of these games are very sophisticated and understand vocabularies as high as 600 words. Be forewarned: it can take *months* to complete a game. They are a lot of fun, but they can consume an enormous amount of time at the workplace. Be sure and restrict game-playing to lunch breaks and after-hours. However, games can be quite useful as ice-breakers when introducing a computer-shy person to the computer for the first time.

Good games for CP/M computers are not very easy to find. If your local dealer doesn't stock them (or can't get them for you) have a look in the computer magazines.

PROGRAMMING LANGUAGES

All computer programs are written in a **programming language**, which contains a set of instructions that tells the computer what to do. When you buy a piece of applications software, it is already written in a programming language. You never have to use the programming language yourself. That's what programmers are for. If you want to learn how to program the computer yourself, you can buy a programming language (which is actually another piece of software) and have at it. You'll also have to buy a couple of books on the subject. Some people have a natural talent for programming and pick it up quickly. Others agonize over it for years and never get very good at it.

The important thing to remember is that if you want to learn how to program your own computer, that's fine. But don't fool yourself into thinking that you can write your own applications program with a week's worth of programming experience. If you want to learn how to program, do it for recreational purposes.

The most popular programming language for beginners is called **BASIC**, which stands for Beginners All-purpose Symbolic Instruction Code. Other languages are **FORTRAN** (used mainly in scientific applications), **COBOL** (used for business applications), **Pascal** (popular with academics), and lots of special purpose languages such as SNOBOL, LISP, Forth, C, PL/1, APL, etc. **Machine language**, sometimes called **assembly language**, is the most basic set of instructions that the computer can understand. Just so you can see how this all fits together: an applications package is written in a programming language which is written in machine language.

WHAT HAVE YOU LEARNED SO FAR?

To start with, you learned that a piece of applications software is what gives the computer its personality. You learned about word processors, spelling checkers, electronic spreadsheets, database managers and accounting packages. You learned that games can be fun, but can also waste a lot of time. You learned the difference between canned and customized software, and that certain types of packages (such as word processors) can be used off-the-shelf, while others, such as accounting packages, will probably need to be customized. You want that customization to be done for you by a professional programmer. You learned that user-friendly software is good to have, but to make sure that the level of user-friendliness can be reduced or turned off altogether. Finally, you learned what a programming language is, and that you don't ever need to use one unless it's just for fun.

Section 4

Buying a Computer

Chapter Twelve

Buying a Computer

Congratulations! You've almost made it through the entire book. The only thing left is to tie together everything you've learned so that you don't feel foolish or afraid when you venture out to buy a computer. This last chapter will be a quick review of some of the things to look for when buying a computer, but first we're going to give you a few tips on selecting a good place to buy a computer.

SHOPPING FOR A COMPUTER STORE

Finding the right place to buy a computer is just as important as finding the right computer. Computers are not like typewriters; you can't just plug them in and start using them. They need to be installed in your place of business, and the people that will use the computer will need to be taught how to use it. If you are going to need custom or customized software, someone is going to have to write it for you. If the computer ever needs service, someone is going to have to come out and fix it. And lastly, someone is going to have to help you determine the right hardware/software combination for you.

All of these functions are the responsibility of the computer store. However, all of the above services may not be included in the basic price of the computer.

If you choose a computer store that is weak in any of these areas, your computer experience may not be a happy one.

Begin your search for a computer store by looking in the yellow pages under "Computer Stores." If your phone book doesn't have such a classification (even the Silicon Valley books didn't until 1981), try "Data Processing Equipment and Supplies." Look at the ads and write down the addresses. Call the store first and ask if it is necessary to make an appointment to see their wares. Some types of stores, called **systems houses**, don't cater to walk-in business, but only sell to buyers of complete systems (you are probably one of these buyers, and a systems house is one of the better places to buy a computer).

Go into the store, armed with the knowledge gained from reading this book, and ask to see a small business computer system. If the salesperson takes you over to a computer and immediately starts to show you the latest shoot-em-up color graphics game, politely restate that you want to see a *business* computer. If that doesn't get you anywhere, excuse yourself and leave. You don't want to buy a computer there.

Well, to be fair, you don't want to buy a computer from that salesperson. If all you can see in the store are the popular personal computers, you probably won't have much luck getting what you want from that store, no matter who the salesperson is. If you see the type of computer you're after, ask to see a salesperson knowledgeable about business systems, or ask to see the manager or owner of the store. If no one can help you, move on to the next store.

A computer store should have a sales staff that can talk to you intelligently about their business systems, and more importantly, about the business problems you expect the computer to solve for you. This is the key. You need a computer store that can help you analyze your computing needs (for now and the future) and help you make the right choice in hardware. They should also be able to help you determine what software you will need. If canned software won't do the trick, they should help you specify modifications to existing packages, or whole new programs (they should know if a whole new program is necessary or not). When you've made your purchase, they should come out to your place of business and set up the computer for you and make sure it works. They should then train you or your designated employees how to use the system. You should also be able to purchase some kind of service contract so that if the computer "goes down" your **downtime** will be as short as possible. As we mentioned earlier, you may have to pay for some or all of these services. Go ahead and pay the money. It will be worth it.

Dealing with the Salespeople

Unfortunately, it's easy for a computer salesperson to quickly get ahead of you when he is describing all the wondrous features of the computer to you. Computer salespeople are often experienced professionals that have been involed with computers for years. As a result, they sometimes forget that customers may not understand some of the jargon. Don't be afraid to ask questions. If there's something you don't understand, ask! Far from getting impatient, the salesperson should be glad to answer questions for you. He should realize that by answering your questions now, a lot of time will be saved by not having to go back over things later. This book was intended to help you deal with all the buzzwords, and give you enough knowledge about computers to keep the salesperson from snowing you. Don't be afraid to carry this book with you into the store. First, the glossary may come in handy, and second, you'll know friendly advice is always close at hand. If you suspect a snow job, brandish the book at the salesperson and threaten to look things up. That should clear the snow.

MAIL ORDER PURCHASING

Generally, it is better to buy a computer from a local dealer than it is to buy one from a mail order house. The mail order discounts may look attractive, but you'll have no one to hold your hand, and believe us, you're going to need that hand holding. Don't expect your local dealer to help you get your mail order system up and running. Certainly don't waste your dealer's time by having them help you specify a system, and then buy it from a mail order discounter. The mail order houses can afford to discount because they don't have to hold your hand (and they won't). If you call the manufacturer for help, don't be surprised if the manufacturer simply refers you to the place where you bought the system. Take our advice and buy your computer from a local establishment that will be there when you need it.

If you live in some remote part of the country (or world) and don't have a local computer dealer, try to buy from a mail order dealer that specializes in systems. They usually won't have discount prices, and will be willing to hold your hand over the telephone.

A WORD OR TWO ABOUT WARRANTIES

Take the time to compare the manufacturer's warranty on the computer system and peripherals. Warranties are particularly important with electromechanical devices, such as disk drives and printers, because they are more likely to break than all-electronic devices such as computer boards. Most manufacturer's warranties require the defective product to be returned to the factory for service. Your dealer may have a "loaner" program, and some manufacturers offer a **board exchange warranty**. This means that, rather than wait for your old board to be repaired, you get a new board to replace the defective one. Some manufacturers guarantee one-day replacement with a board exchange warranty, which can really minimize down-time. Expect to pay a premium for boards that carry this kind of warranty.

A FEW THINGS TO REMEMBER TO LOOK FOR

By now you should know what to look for in the basic computing hardware, peripherals and software. A few points are worth repeating, though. You probably ought to buy a modular computer (preferably an IEEE 696/S-100 computer) that can be expanded as your computing needs increase (and they will). You will need at least two 8-inch floppy disk drives, preferably double-sided, double density. Make sure the enclosures for the mainframe and disk drives are well constructed and have adequate cooling. You will need a terminal and a printer. Remember that if you are not going to use the terminal yourself, take the person who will be using it "terminal shopping." The printer you need depends on the type of computing you will be doing. If you're going to do lots of word processing, you'll need a letter quality printer.

You want a computer that uses the CP/M operating system. Applications software should be **CP/M compatible**. Some applications software can be used off-the-shelf, such as word processors and electronic spreadsheets, but some software will need to be customized for your application. If you need a multi-user computer system, you will need a multi-user operating system, such as MP/M.

Finally, you'll need to choose a good computer store or systems house from which to buy your computer. A good computer store or systems house should have the following:

1) A sales staff knowledgeable in business computing applications and systems.
2) A programmer to customize software for you.
3) A technician who can fix the computer if it breaks.
4) The ability to set the computer up at your place of business and train you in its operation.
5) A service contract available for the hardware you buy.
6) Most importantly, a system to demonstrate to you.

Well, there you have it: a basic tour of the elements that make up computing systems. Now it's time to sit down with the knowledgeable salespeople at your local computer store and have a good talk. Now that you've gained all the knowledge in this book, with a little bit of advice and training, you'll be well on your way to improving—and simplifying—your life with the help of that magical device, the computer.

Section 5

Glossary

Glossary of Common Terms

Acoustic coupler – The part of a modem that transmits data to the handset of a common telephone, but not the modem itself. See *acoustically coupled* and *modem*.

Acoustically coupled – An acoustically coupled modem connects a computer or terminal to the phone lines. It sends and receives tones by means of a speaker and microphone that are placed next to the handset of a common telephone. See *direct connect* and *modem*.

All-in-one computer – A computer that contains the CPU, memory, screen, keyboard and disk drives all in one cabinet.

Answer mode – The ability of a modem to accept (answer) an incoming call from another modem. See *modem*.

Applications program – Software that allows the computer to perform specific applications or tasks, such as word processing, accounting or economic forecasting.

Applications software – See *applications program*.

ASCII (pronounced as'key) – Abbreviation for American Standard Code for Information Interchange. This is a standard code for the computer representation of the various characters, numbers, punctuation marks and other symbols available on a standard typewriter-like keyboard. Most peripherals use ASCII, which ensures that any given character will always be the same on different peripherals.

Assembly language–The human readable form of *machine language*. See *machine language*.

Auto-answer–The ability of a modem to answer the phone line in response to an incoming call. See *modem*.

Auto-dial–The ability of a modem to dial a phone number. See *modem*.

Backup or Back-up–Noun: A duplicate set of data to be used in case the original is lost, destroyed or accidentally altered. For example, the information on one diskette may be copied over to another diskette; this second diskette is called the *backup* copy. Back-up copies are often stored off-premises so that fire, flood, theft or other problems will not cause important data to be lost forever. Verb: The process of creating a duplicate set of data to be used in case the original is lost, destroyed or accidentally altered.

BASIC–A programming language that is widely used in microcomputers because of its English-like structure and ease of use. Developed originally as a programming language for beginners, it stands for Beginners All-purpose Symbolic Instruction Code. See *programming language*.

Baud rate–The measure of speed at which information is transferred, expressed in bits per second. Dividing the baud rate by ten equals the approximate number of characters transferred from one device to another in one second. See *bits per second*.

BDOS–The part of CP/M that is identical (never changes) from system to system. BDOS stands for Basic Disk Operating System. The BDOS and the BIOS make up the CP/M operating system. See *CP/M*, *BIOS* and *operating system*.

BIOS – The part of CP/M that needs to be specially configured for each type of computer system, usually done by the manufacturer of that system. BIOS stands for Basic Input/Output System. The BIOS and the BDOS make up the CP/M operating system. See *BDOS* and *CP/M*.

Bit – An abbreviation for *binary digit*. The bit is the most fundamental unit of information that a computer can accept. A bit has two states, called "1" and "0" (one and zero). Thus, a single bit can represent a yes/no type of statement. Groups of bits are used to represent more complex statements (such as a character). The most common grouping of bits is called a *byte*, which consists of eight bits. See *byte*, *eight bit computer*, *sixteen bit computer* and *word*.

Bits per second – A measure of the number of bits transferred from one device to another in one second. See *baud rate*.

BPS – Abbreviation for bits per second. See *bits per second*.

Board exchange warranty – A warranty that provides a customer with a new replacement board when the original needs fixing instead of having to wait for the original board to be repaired.

Buffer – A small amount of memory, usually in a printer, that allows the computer to send data to the printer at a rate which is faster than the printer can print the characters. The buffer holds the characters for printing.

Bug – An error in a program.

Bus – A series of electrical pathways which take information and power from place to place within a computer system. Typically located on a motherboard. See *motherboard* and *IEEE 696/S-100*.

Byte – The name given to a group of eight bits. In ASCII code, each character is represented by one byte. See *bit*.

Canned software – Pre-packaged software (usually an applications program) designed to work with many standard computer systems. See *applications program*.

Capacity – When describing memory, capacity refers to the amount of information that the memory can store, usually expressed in K bytes or megabytes. See *byte*, *K byte* and *megabyte*.

Carbon ribbon – Used with printers to produce extremely sharp characters with excellent definition. Much the same as carbon ribbons used with electric typewriters, they make only one pass through the printer before being discarded. See *fabric ribbon*.

Cartridge tape system – A system for storing data on a cartridge of magnetic tape. Usually used for backup purposes, rather than for main storage. Note: A cartridge tape system is not the same as a cassette tape system such as is used in a home stereo. See *backup*.

Cathode ray tube – More commonly known as a CRT, the picture tube in a terminal, functionally similar to those used in standard televisions.

Cell – A field of data, manipulated by a spreadsheet simulator program. The spreadsheet program deals with data in rows and columns; the intersection of a row and column is the cell. See *spreadsheet simulator*.

Central processing unit – Usually abbreviated CPU, the section of a computer system responsible for controlling and manipulating (add, subtract, compare, etc.) the flow of data in the computer system. Can refer either to the actual CPU chip or the circuit board that contains it. See *CPU board* and *CPU chip*.

Centronics interface – A common parallel interface for low cost printers.

Character – A single letter, number, symbol, space or punctuation mark.

Characters per second – When referring to printers, a measure of the average number of characters that the printer can print in one second.

Circuit board – A flat, thin piece of fiberglass/epoxy material on which the various electronic components mount. The circuit board also provides electrical pathways, called traces, that electrically connect these various components.

COBOL – A programming language used mainly in business programs. See *programming language*.

Command – Something you instruct the computer to do, such as run a program.

Computer enclosure – The housing or cabinet for the computer boards, typically including a motherboard and power supply. See *motherboard* and *power supply*.

Constant voltage transformer – A transformer converts the voltage coming out of the wall to lower voltage suitable for powering computer boards. A constant voltage transformer maintains a constant voltage to the computer boards, even when the wall voltage fluctuates over a very wide range (such as during a brown-out).

CP/M – Written by Digital Research, Inc., CP/M stands for Control Program for Microcomputers and is the most popular operating system for microcomputers. Different versions of CP/M are available for both 8 and 16 bit computers. See *operating system* and *MP/M*.

CP/M compatible – Software designed to operate in conjunction with the CP/M operating system. See *CP/M* and *operating system*.

CPS – Abbreviation for characters per second. See *characters per second*.

CPU – Abbreviation for central processing unit. See *central processing unit*, *CPU chip* and *CPU board*.

CPU board – The circuit board that contains the CPU chip and associated components. See *central processing unit* and *CPU chip*.

CPU chip – The actual microprocessor IC (integrated circuit) that forms the basis of the computer system. See *central processing unit* and *IC*.

Crash – A word used to describe the (usually fatal) failure of a program or piece of hardware.

CRT – Abbreviation for cathode ray tube, the actual picture tube in a terminal. CRT is also used to refer to the whole terminal. See *cathode ray tube* and *terminal*.

Customize – The process of altering a piece of general-purpose software or hardware to enhance its performance, usually to fit a specific user's needs.

Cut sheet feeder – See *single sheet feeder*.

CV transformer – See *constant voltage transformer*.

Daisy wheel – Conceptually similar to the "golf ball" found in many office typewriters, the daisy wheel contains all standard alphabet characters, numbers and punctuation marks. A mechanism in the printer rotates the daisy wheel to the proper position and a hammer strikes one of the "petals" of the daisy causing a character to impact the paper through a ribbon. See *daisy wheel printer*.

Daisy wheel printer – A printer that uses daisy wheels to produce highly legible print quality. See *daisy wheel* and *letter quality printer*.

Data – The information being processed (or about to be processed) by the computer.

Database – A collection of data that the computer may access, such as a mailing list, inventory, etc.

Database management system – A piece of applications software used to efficiently extract and manipulate the information contained in a database. Commonly abbreviated DBMS. See *database*.

Daughter board – A circuit board that plugs into a motherboard. See *motherboard*.

DBMS – Abbreviation for Database Management System.

Detachable keyboard – A keyboard that is not built into the same case as the screen of a terminal. Connects to the terminal with a cable, and allows greater flexibility in positioning of the keyboard/screen. See *terminal*.

Direct connect – A type of modem that connects directly to the phone lines, rather than coupling into the phone lines through less efficient acoustical means. Allows the modem to dial and answer on the line. See *modem*, *auto-answer*, *auto-dial* and *acoustically coupled*.

Direct memory access – A process whereby peripheral devices can access the memory of the computer directly, without intervention of the CPU, thus speeding up operation. Commonly abbreviated DMA.

Disk controller – A board residing in the computer's mainframe that handles the flow of data to and from the computer's RAM and disk drives.

Disk drive – The mechanism that holds magnetic storage media (floppy diskette, hard disk platter, etc.) and causes it to rotate. Also handles the actual reading and writing of the data to and from the disk.

Disk drive enclosure – A box designed to hold one or more disk drives and a power supply.

Diskette – Short for floppy diskette. See *floppy diskette*.

DOS – Abbreviation for Disk Operating System. See *operating system*.

Dot matrix printer – A relatively fast printer that forms characters with a matrix of little dots, usually not as readable as a letter quality printer. See *multiple pass printing*.

Double density – A diskette that holds twice as much data as a single density diskette. Not the same as double-sided.

Double-sided – A diskette that has data stored on both sides of the media, thereby doubling the amount of data stored. Not the same as double density.

Down-time – The amount of time the computer is not working ("down").

Draft quality printer – A printer (usually dot matrix) that produces print quality suitable for drafts of reports, manuscripts, etc., but not the final product. See *letter quality printer.*

Dual density – Capable of operating in single and double density modes, not to be confused with double density.

Dynamic memory – Memory that will lose its data unless it is constantly "refreshed." Characterized by low cost and relatively complex circuitry to make it work properly. See *static memory.*

Edge connector – The part of the motherboard that provides the electrical and mechanical connections to the daughter board. See *motherboard* and *daughter board.*

8 Bit CPU – A CPU that transfers its data 8 bits at a time. Usually not as powerful as a 16 bit CPU. See *bit*, *CPU* and *16 Bit CPU.*

Electronic spreadsheet – See *spreadsheet simulator.*

Electrostatic printer – A type of dot matrix printer that forms characters on a special, aluminized paper. It burns tiny dots through the aluminized surface by means of an electrostatic discharge. See *dot matrix printer.*

Ergonomics – The science of designing equipment so that it is easy and pleasing for people to use.

Fabric ribbon – A type of printer ribbon, usually made out of a nylon fabric, that is impregnated with ink. It can make pass after pass through the printer until the ink eventually dries out. Its print quality is not as good as a carbon ribbon. See *carbon ribbon*.

Fan-fold paper – A continuous string of individual sheets of paper where each sheet is separated by a line of perforations. Sometimes referred to as Z-fold paper.

Floppy disk drive – See *disk drive*.

Floppy diskette – A disk-shaped, thin piece of mylar, coated with magnetic particles, that rotates inside a paper jacket. The storage media used with floppy disk systems.

Forms tractor – A device which accurately feeds, aligns and automatically advances continuous forms or paper into the printer.

FORTRAN – A programming language used mainly in scientific applications. See *programming language*.

Hard copy – The output from a printer. The "soft copy" is the one on the screen.

Hard disk system – A mass storage system capable of holding huge amounts of data (hundreds of megabytes as of this writing).

Hardware – The computer itself, and any other devices or machines required to make the computer system work (such as a terminal, printer, etc.).

IC – Abbreviation for integrated circuit. See *integrated circuit*.

IEEE 696/S-100 – The name of a standard, developed by the *Institute of Electrical and Electronic Engineers*. It insures compatibility between all computing products designed to this standard.

Impact printer – Any printer that makes a character by impacting the paper through a ribbon, just like an ordinary office typewriter.

Input – Noun: That which is put in, for example, the data that is fed into a computer. Verb: The process of feeding data into a computer. See *output*.

Input devices – These accept data from the outside world, and convert that data into a form that the computer can use. See *output devices*.

Input/Output devices – Commonly abbreviated *I/O devices*. This term refers to combinations of input and output devices.

Install – The process of taking a piece of general-purpose software and tailoring it to work with specific types of terminals, printers and computers.

Integrate – The process of putting various components together to form a harmonious computer system. Usually accomplished by a computer store or *systems integrator*.

Integrated circuit – Commonly abbreviated IC. An electronic device that replaces dozens, hundreds or even thousands of standard electronic components. The IC is responsible for miniaturizing the computer to such an extent that computing power that formerly took up hundreds of cubic feet of space can now fit unobtrusively on a desktop.

Integrated system – A computer system that has been put together into a "standard" configuration. A system is *pre-integrated* if the computer manufacturer does the integrating. See *integrate*.

Interface – Noun: A circuit or other piece of hardware that is used to connect computers and peripherals together. Verb: The process of connecting computer and peripherals together.

I/O – Abbreviation for Input/Output.

I/O board – A board that plugs into a computer to allow the computer and the outside world to "talk" to each other. See *interface*.

I/O devices – See *Input/Output devices*.

I/O port – That part of a computer, physical or electrical, where peripherals are connected. Called a "port" because that's where data enters and leaves the computer. Also see *Input/Output devices, interface* and *I/O board*.

Jacket – The stiff paper container that holds a floppy diskette.

K – Abbreviation for the number 1024, actually an abbreviation of the prefix *kilo*.

K byte – 1024 bytes.

Kilobyte – See *K byte*.

KSR – Abbreviation for Keyboard Send and Receive. Used to describe a printer that also contains a keyboard, allowing the printer/keyboard combination to be used as a terminal. See *RO*.

Language – See *programming language*.

Letter quality printer – A printer that is capable of producing print quality comparable to a standard office typewriter. See *draft quality printer*.

Line filter – An electronic device used to keep interference, caused by machinery and things such as fluorescent lights, out of the computer. Such interference (or noise) is usually transmitted on the power lines.

Line voltage – The AC voltage that comes out of a standard wall socket.

Load – The process of putting data into the computer's memory, usually from a mass storage system.

Machine language – The most basic form of instruction that the computer can understand.

Magnetic tape – One of the earliest forms of mass storage. Reels or cartridges of magnetic tape, very similar to audio or video tape, are used to store large amounts of data. See *mass storage system*.

Mail-merging – The process of automatically printing form letters with names and addresses from a mailing list file. Used to seemingly personalize a form letter.

Mainframe – The combination of CPU, memory and I/O boards in a computer enclosure.

Mainframe computer – Different than the mainframe of a small computer system, a mainframe computer is the term used to refer to a very large computer installation.

Mass storage system/memory – Typically stores more data than a computer's RAM, but cannot be accessed directly by the CPU. Thus, data to be stored in a mass storage system must first be placed in RAM, and then transferred to the mass storage system. Likewise, data in a mass storage system must be transferred to RAM before the CPU can use it. The most common forms of mass storage systems are the floppy and hard disk systems. See *RAM*, *floppy disk system* and *hard disk system*.

M byte – Abbreviation for megabyte.

Megabyte – 1024K bytes, which totals slightly more than one million bytes. See *K byte*.

Memory – That part of a computer that stores data, either temporarily or permanently. See *RAM*.

Microprocessor – The central processing unit of a computer system, usually contained in one IC. See *CPU*, *CPU chip* and *integrated circuit*.

Mini-floppy – The name given to a 5¼-inch floppy disk system or diskette. See headings under *floppy*.

MPU – Abbreviation for Micro Processing Unit. See *CPU chip*.

Modem – Short for modulator/demodulator; a device that allows a computer or terminal to transfer data to a similarly equipped computer or terminal over telephone lines.

Modular computer system – A computer system where all of its various components (CPU, memory, etc.) are contained on separate circuit boards, allowing total system flexibility.

Motherboard – A circuit board containing connectors into which daughter boards are plugged. The motherboard contains electrical pathways that connect the daughter boards together, allowing them to work as a unified team.

MP/M – A multi-user operating system, written by Digital Research Inc., that allows the use of CP/M compatible programs. See *multi-user operating system* and *CP/M*.

Multiple pass printing – A technique used on better dot matrix printers to get higher quality characters. The print head makes one pass, the paper is moved slightly and another pass is made. This tends to fill in the spaces between the dots. See *dot matrix printer*.

Multi-user operating system – A type of operating system software that allows several people to use a computer at the same time. See *operating system*.

Multi-user system – A computer system designed to allow more than one user on the system at a time.

Negative pressurization – When the cooling of an enclosure is accomplished by pulling air through the vent holes and pushing it out through the fan hole, creating a negative pressure inside the enclosure. Not desirable. See *positive pressurization*.

Non-removable – A hard disk platter that always stays within the hard disk drive. See *platter*.

Non-volatile – Data that remains when power is turned off. See *volatile*.

Null modem cable – A special cable used for connecting modems to computers whose serial interfaces are designed for terminals, not modems.

Number-crunching – Repetitive series of mathematical calculations.

Numeric pad – A separate set of keys, arranged in a 10-key adding machine format, usually located to the right of the standard keyboard on a terminal. Numeric pad is provided in addition to the "normal" number keys at the top of the keyboard. Useful for entering large amounts of numeric data.

OASIS – A multi-user operating system, not capable of using CP/M compatible software. See *multi-user operating system* and *CP/M*.

Operating system – A piece of software that allows the terminal, printer, computer and mass storage system to work together as a unit.

Originate mode modem – A modem that is capable only of being on the originating end of the phone line. It cannot answer a call from another modem. See *answer mode modem* and *modem*.

Originate/answer mode modem – A modem capable of both originating and receiving a data transfer on the phone lines. See *modem*.

Output – Noun: That which comes out of a computer or peripheral. For example, the characters on a printer's paper. Verb: The process of sending information out of a computer.

Output devices – These are devices by which a computer transfers its information to the outside world. For example, the printer is an output device that prints computer data in an easily readable form.

Parallel interfacing – A particular method of interfacing peripherals and computers, where each bit of information has its own wire. Not as common as the serial RS-232C interface. See *serial interfacing*.

Parallel port – The physical or electrical port of a computer where parallel data enters and leaves. See *I/O port*.

Pascal – A programming language, popular for teaching programming, usually at the university level. See *programming language*.

Peripherals – Input and output devices that connect to computers. Terminals, printers and modems are examples of peripherals.

Platter—That part of a hard disk drive that actually stores the information. Similar in function to a floppy diskette, but is rigid or "hard."

Polarizing filter—An accessory for terminal screens to reduce glare.

Positive pressurization—The cooling of an enclosure, accomplished by pulling air in through the fan hole and pushing it out through the vent holes, creating a positive pressure in the enclosure. Recommended because it allows the use of an air filter. See *negative pressurization.*

Power supply—That part of a computer which takes the wall voltages and converts them into voltages that the computer uses.

Pre-configured system—See *integrated system.*

Pre-integrated system—See *integrated system.*

Printer—A peripheral used to put computer data on paper.

Print head—In a dot matrix printer, the part that contains the mechanism for impacting the ribbon and paper.

Printout—The paper that comes out of the printer (that has already been printed on).

Program—Noun: A set of instructions designed to tell the computer to perform a specific task. For example, a word processing program instructs the computer to perform complex editing and printing functions. Verb: The process of devising a set of instructions designed to make the computer perform a specific task.

Programming language—The language used to write programs for computers. A programming language is a piece of software, but is also used to write pieces of software, called applications programs. See *applications program*, *program* and *software.*

Quad density – Another name for double-sided, double density storage media and systems. Gives four times the storage of single-sided, single density.

RAM – RAM is an acronym for Random Access Memory, which is the memory inside a computer that the CPU can access directly. Also see *memory* and *mass storage system*.

Read – The process of transferring pre-stored data from storage devices into memory.

Regulating – The process of stabilizing a varying input voltage for more reliable operation and freedom from brown-outs. Usually accomplished by the power supply. See *constant voltage transformer* and *power supply*.

Relational DBMS – A database management system that allows sorting through data and extracting only those items that meet certain criteria. See *database management system*.

Removable media – Media of a storage system that can be removed from the disk drive.

RO – Stands for Receive Only. Refers to most printers which can only receive data from the computer (they have no keyboard). See *KSR*.

ROM – Stands for Read Only Memory. A type of memory whose contents can be read but not written to. A non-volatile storage medium for some types of programs.

RS-232C serial interface – The most common (and standard) way to interface peripherals and computers. Most peripherals utilize an RS-232C interface.

Save – The process of transferring data into mass storage.

Semi-modular computer – A computer that contains most of its important parts (CPU, memory, etc.) on one circuit board; but also contains some method of increasing its capabilities, usually by the use of expansion slots. See *single-board computer* and *slots*.

Serial port – That place, either physical or electrical, where data enters and leaves the computer one bit at a time. Also see *RS-232* and *parallel port*.

Shell – A piece of software that "hides" the internals of a program from the user, and instead presents an easy to use "face." The shell is written around the original piece of software.

Shielding – The quality of an enclosure or motherboard intended to reduce electrical noise.

Single-board computer – A computer that contains all its circuitry on one board. Not expandable.

Single density – A particular diskette format used with early floppy disk systems, storing a minimum amount of data. See *double density*.

Single sheet feeder – An accessory for printers designed to feed one sheet of paper at a time, such as letterhead stock, into a printer.

Single-sided – Floppy disk media or system that can store data on only one side of the media. See *double-sided*.

Single-user system – A computer designed for only one person to use at a time.

Single-user operating system – An operating system designed to accept only one user at a time. See *multi-user operating system*.

16 Bit computer – A computer system that is capable of processing data sixteen bits at a time, potentially twice as fast as an eight bit system. Sixteen bit systems can usually accommodate more RAM than eight bit systems, making some applications more efficient.

Slots – Another name for the edge connectors on a motherboard, where daughter boards plug in. Some semi-modular computers contain small motherboards with a few slots, intended for expansion of the computer's capabilities. See *motherboard*.

Software – Unlike hardware, software is not an electronic product and does not perform any physical work. Rather, software is a set of instructions that tells the hardware how to complete a particular task. See *program* and *hardware*.

Special function board – Computer boards designed to perform highly specialized tasks, such as timing events, keeping track of the time and date, processing numeric data at very high speeds, etc.

Spelling checker – An applications program that searches text stored in a computer system for misspelled words by comparing words against a large dictionary, which is also stored in the computer.

Spreadsheet simulator – An applications program that allows financial forecasting and similar applications to be performed using a large electronic grid of numbers and formulas. The grid is "live": if you change one number, the rest of the grid is updated instantly to reflect the change. The terminal screen provides a movable window on the grid. Also called an electronic spreadsheet.

Static memory – A type of RAM that retains its data indefinitely, as long as power is applied, with no further intervention from the memory circuitry. Preferred in modular systems over dynamic memory, which needs complicated "refreshing" circuitry in order to retain its data. See *dynamic memory*.

Store – See *save*.

Systems house – A type of computer store that only sells complete systems, and usually only sells upgrade products and accessories to previous systems customers. Usually does a better job of installing a business computer system than a general-purpose computer store.

Terminal – The main communications device between the computer and the user. Typically includes a TV-like screen which shows data being entered into (or output from) the computer, and a typewriter-like keyboard.

Termination circuitry – Circuitry included on better motherboards, designed to provide faster and more reliable operation of the computer system.

Text editor – An applications program designed to allow easy manipulation of text with a terminal, usually not as sophisticated as a word processing program. See *word processor*.

Thimble printer – Similar in function to a daisy wheel printer, but uses type wheels in the shape of a thimble instead of a daisy. See *daisy wheel printer*.

Time-sharing – The process of allowing many users to share a single computer, all at the same time. See *multi-user operating system*.

Traces – The electrical pathways on circuit boards that connect the various electronic components together.

Transformer – A device used to convert the voltage from the wall socket down to a voltage usable by the computer. The transformer is part of the power supply. See *constant voltage transformer* and *power supply*.

UNIX – An operating system, for both single and multiple users, that is popular in the academic community. Not available for eight bit computer systems.

Up-gradability – The ability of a computer system to be changed as the user's needs change. Possible only with modular and semi-modular systems.

User – A person using a computer.

User-friendly – The quality of a piece of software that makes it very easy for the inexperienced person to use.

VDT – Abbreviation for Video Display Terminal.

Video display terminal – A term originally used to differentiate between terminals that used paper and terminals that used screens for output. Not used much any more because the majority of terminals use a screen. See *terminal*.

Volatile – Memory is described as being volatile if it loses its data when power is interrupted. A computer's RAM is usually volatile. See *non-volatile*.

Word processor – A piece of applications software that allows the easy and powerful manipulation of text using a terminal's screen and keyboard, and sophisticated printing of that text on a printer.

Write – The process of transferring data into memory or into a mass storage system.

Z-fold paper – See *fan-fold paper*.

Index

Note: Definitions for all of the words contained in this index will also be found in the glossary.

Trademark Acknowledgements

Apple II, III   Apple Computer, Inc.
Asteroids   Atari, Inc.
Centronics   Centronics Data Computer
                    Corporation
CompuPro   Godbout Electronics
CP/M, MP/M   Digital Research, Inc.
8080 chip   Intel Corporation
IBM Selectric   IBM Corporation
OASIS   Phase One, Inc.
The Source   Source Telecomputing Corporation
Space Invaders   Atari, Inc.
UNIX   Bell Laboratories
Z80 Chip   Zilog Corporation
Zenith Z-100   Zenith Data Systems Corporation

About the Author

Mark Garetz graduated from Cal State Fullerton, majoring in telecommunications. He is self-taught in the subject of digital electronics and microprocessors. Mark is the author of many articles on microcomputing which have appeared in Creative Computing, Byte, ComputerWorld, Kilobaud and Dr. Dobb's Journal. Mr. Garetz was also a Contributing Editor for InfoWorld magazine. He is the foremost designer working with the S-100 BUS, and is the Chairman of the IEEE 696S-100 standard committee. Along with Mr. Garetz's many interests and talents, he is the owner and President of Micronics, a microcomputer consulting firm. Currently he is working at Compu-Pro, a division of Godbout Electronics.